Best of
CANADA

Over seven thousand kilometres separate these two photographs,
Canada's bookends if you like. Were it not for the pea-soup fog rolling in off the
North Atlantic, you would be the first person on the continent of North America to
see the sunrise if you were standing near that lighthouse on Cape Spear.
And the enchanting, mist-tinged beach on the west coast of far-off
Vancouver Island would offer you Canada's last snapshot of that same sun
as it dipped into the Pacific Ocean on its never-er
breathing life into all living things on the

D1404149

MAGIC LIGHT PUBLISH
OTTAWA

This satellite image of Canada was created by mosaicing hundreds of pieces of cloud-free data taken from many different images photographed over a period of about 4 years. These pieces were then colour balanced and blended to remove any seams between them and the whole was adjusted blended

Morning mist over Long Beach, Pacific Rim National Park.
A. Cornellier/Parks Canada/10.104.03.18.106

Canada, from sea to sea to sea—pacific to Arctic to Atlantic—you could spend a lifetime travelling this vast country, from village to village, town to town, city to city, east to west, north to south, river to river and lake to lake.

Through mountain prairie, dune, glacier, barren land, badlands and tundra, explore fjord, meadow, valley, forest, coast, wetlands and icebergs—all framing a wealth of equally varied urban landscapes. Step back in time to where dinosaurs roamed, before the last great ice age carved out a land that would become the Canada you see in this photo, land that offered an abundance of natural resources that would sustain the lives of all who lived here since the ice retreated some 10,000 years ago.

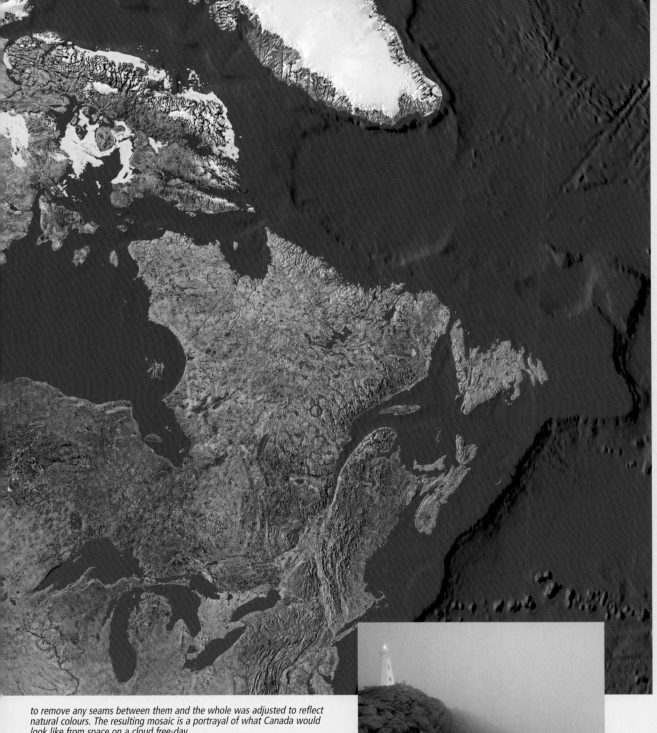

These two pages represent all this, and more! Canada is renowned the world over as a country of remarkable beauty and natural wonder. This grand mosaic is held together by a people who are as varied as the landscapes that shaped them.

Cape Spear lighthouse shrouded in typical Newfoundland fog rolling in off the Atlantic Ocean.

From this huge country—with all its natural wonder and history— we've selected a variety of photos to reflect the *Best of Canada*. It is by no means a complete picture (try to fit over 7000 kilometres into one book without resorting to a satellite camera view) but we believe these 160 pages will portray for you the essence and spirit of this country in her Sunday best, from sea to sea to sea.

Best of
CANADA

By: Jeff Hutcheson
Photography: John McQuarrie

Copyright: 2014 John McQuarrie

Published by: John McQuarrie Photography
                     Magic Light Publishing
                     192 Bruyere Street
                     Ottawa, Ontario
                     Canada   K1N 5E1

                     TEL: (613) 241-1833
                     FAX: (613) 241-2085
                     mcq@magma.ca
Bulk Sales Enquires (800) 843-0908

Design   John McQuarrie
Printing   Friesens Corporation, Altona, Manitoba

Printed and bound in Canada

National Library of Canada Cataloguing in Publication

Hutcheson, Jeff
         Best of Canada / Jeff Hutcheson.
Includes index.
ISBN 1-894673-11-5

         1. Canada--Pictorial works. I. Title.

FC59.H88 2003   971.064'8'0222
C2003-901715-X
F1017.H88 2003

Title page (top): Cape Spear lighthouse shrouded in typical Newfoundland fog rolling in off the Atlantic Ocean.

Title page (bottom) Morning mist over Long Beach, Pacific Rim National Park. A. Cornellier/Parks Canada/10.104.03.18.106

Previous page: Members of the Royal Canadian Mounted Police's world-renowned Musical Ride conclude each performance with their signature "Charge".

Dawn launch of Canada Geese near Lone Butte, British Columbia.

CONTENTS

Canada is made up of ten provinces and three northern territories. Each of them has tourism offices that will be happy to provide you with maps and a wealth of information to assist with your trip planning. To further assist you, we have noted of the province beside the page numbers throughout most of the book.

But this is not a guide book—it's more of a highlight tour designed to showcase many of Canada's most popular attractions and destinations. As you journey through these pages we hope you will be inspired to visit some of our favourites and in the process, discover a few of your own.

Bon Voyage! Jeff

Additional Photography

J. David Andrews	J.A. Kraulis
Mike Beedell	Randy Lincks
J. F. Bergeron	Wayne Lynch
Daryl Benson	Ian MacNeil
J. Bicknell	Mike Macri
Gary Black	P. McCloskey
Bill Brooks	P. Mercier
Peter Christopher	Freeman Patterson
A. Cornellier	J. Pleau
John de Visser	Alec Pytlowany
Miles Ertman	Pierre St-Jacques
Janet Foster	Dale Sanders
T. Hall	Greg Stott
Sherman Hines	Dale Wilson

Pounding surf at Cape Spear near St. John's Newfoundland.

Newfoundland and Labrador

CAPE SPEAR

North America starts here! Located just 20 minutes south of the provincial capital of St. John's, Cape Spear is the easternmost point of North America. It is an awesome feeling to stand with the Atlantic Ocean at your back and realize everyone else on the continent is west of you! And you can see the sunrise here before anyone else in North America!

There are actually two lighthouses here. A newer concrete one (left) functions automatically while the old one (inset photos, right) has been restored to its 1839 appearance and shows how a lightkeeper and his family might have lived in the mid-19th century. The Visitor Centre contains exhibits on the history of lighthouses and the tradition of lightkeeping. The site is surrounded by spectacular scenery and wildlife such as whales, seabirds and icebergs in season

This rugged, rocky shoreline is typical of the province. Step right to the edge of the cliff, with the Atlantic at your feet, and ponder the fact that you are closer to Ireland's Cape Clear, than to Thunder Bay Ontario. Newfoundland and Labrador, a province so unique that it has its own time zone, did not become a part of Canada until 1949. While tourists are drawn here from all over the world, the locals come to pick partridge berries for their famous jams and jellies.

But be prepared! This part of the country generally gets fog about 150 days of the year, and if the sun is shining, count on a very brisk and bracing wind!

Cape Spear lighthouse shrouded in typical Newfoundland fog rolling in off the Atlantic Ocean and (below) under a beautiful afternoon sun.

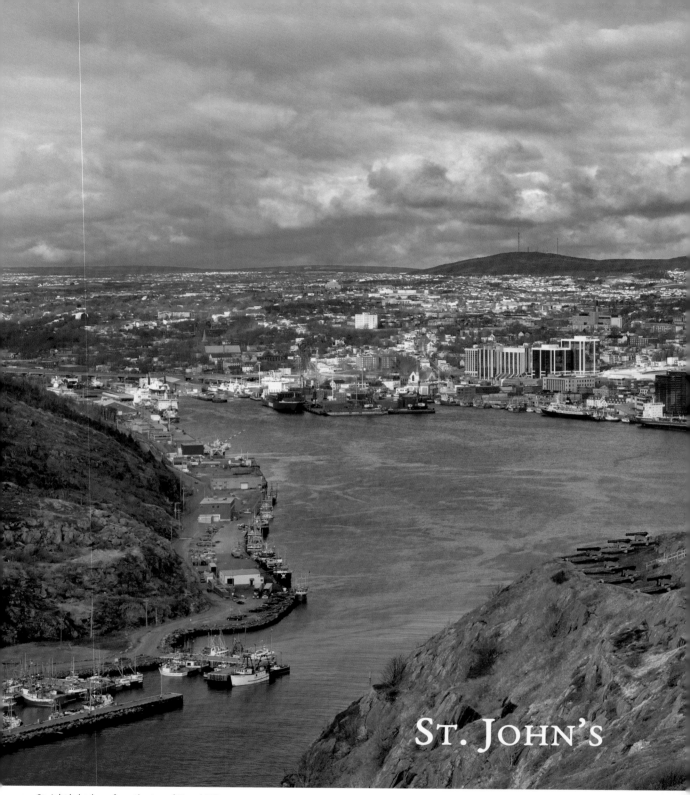

ST. JOHN'S

St. John's harbour from the top of Signal Hill.

Welcome to the oldest city in North America, St. John's, the capital of Newfoundland and Labrador, established as a settlement over 500 years ago. The history of the city is everywhere.

The spectacular natural harbour was home to 40 vessels, 40 years before the Mayflower landed at Plymouth Rock. *The Mayflower* actually stopped for fresh water and food at Renews, a village on the Irish Loop south of St. John's, on her maiden voyage to Plymouth Rock.

Tour boat Scademia.

In 1901, at Signal Hill, with the simple word "Hello", Marconi ushered in the information age by receiving the first transatlantic wireless transmission. But the name "Signal Hill", has its origins in the fact that – long before Marconi – the British used the site for a system of flags to 'signal' an approaching enemy.

I had the chance once to pilot the schooner Scademia (above) in through the narrows. The captain asked if I knew the difference between sailing into the harbour now, as opposed to when the first European visitors did it five hundred years ago. I didn't, and his answer: "No difference": It's true!

Colourful St. John's has many unique joys, like shopping in the oldest store on the oldest street in the oldest city in North America. Nobody comes to this city without visiting Water Street.

Water Street looking west from the foot of McBride's Hill in the 1880s.
City of St. John's Archives, (01-11-008)

The Barbour Living Heritage Village in Newtown, with its many historic buildings, is beautifully situated on a point of land surrounded by small natural harbours and channels (called "tickles") that resemble canals, between the many islands.

The salt-cod fishery was the backbone of Newfoundland and Labrador's economy for much of the 20th century. It encompassed three branches: an inshore fishery off the island's coast, a summer Labrador fishery, and an offshore bank fishery.

Advances in harvesting and processing technology after the Second World War resulted in the gradual industrialization of Newfoundland and Labrador's fisheries. Inshore fishers increasingly used diesel-powered longliners instead of small open boats, while trawlers (also known as draggers) replaced schooners in the bank fishery. More efficient nets, tracking devices, and other gear allowed workers to harvest more fish than ever before, while stronger boats allowed them to remain at sea for longer periods of time. As fishing technology became more efficient, the industry became less sustainable. Decades of overfishing severely depleted cod stocks until they collapsed in the 1990s. The Canadian government imposed a moratorium on the northern cod fishery in 1992, which put about 30,000 people in Newfoundland and Labrador out of work and ended an almost 500-year-old industry.

Jenny Higgins
Newfoundland and Labrador Heritage Web Site Project
www.heritage.nf.ca

Dwyer Fishing Premises in Tilting, on Fogo Island

The stage (Newfoundland term referring to wharf and buildings associated with fishing) is an original part of the Dwyer Fishing Premises in Tilting, on Fogo Island. It won the Southcott Award in 2000, for excellence in the preservation of the architectural heritage of Newfoundland and Labrador. Inside the stage you will find all the items necessary for the processing of fish by hand such as a splitting table, cod liver oil barrel and a puncheon barrel.

Battle Harbour

View of Battle Harbour from Great Caribou Island.

Once the site of a thriving salt fish, salmon and seal processing complex, Battle Harbour was the economic and social centre of the entire coast, known to one and all as the unofficial capital of Labrador. The salt fish plantation at Battle Harbour was established by the firm of John Slade and Company of Poole, England in the 1770s. The Slade premises became the major base for the region's fisheries. The site was operated by several companies until it was abandoned with the collapse of the cod fishery in the early 1990s.

Eclipsed in recent decades by changing economies and settlement patterns, the former glory of Battle Harbour has now been revived. Six years of research and painstaking architectural restoration have breathed new life into this unique historic place.

Through the efforts of the Battle Harbour Historic Trust, the village of Battle Harbour is now a living commemoration of the life and society created there by Newfoundlanders and Labradoreans during the 18th, 19th and 20th centuries.

Once the luxurious residence of the fishing merchants, this beautiful house is now the Battle Harbour Inn.

Battle Harbour General Store is a prime example of the old-fashioned shop common to coastal communities in days gone by.

L'ANSE AUX MEADOWS

In the past four to five thousand years, many people have lived at l'Anse aux Meadows. Some stayed longer than others. Among these people was a small group of Norse sailors. The remains of their camp, discovered in 1960 by Helge and Anne Stine Ingstad, is the oldest known European settlement in the New World.

Reconstructed Viking settlement.

L'Anse aux Meadows, the centrepiece of what Newfoundlanders refer to as Viking country, is located at the top of the Great Northern Peninsula. The area is remote and your journey to this national historic site will take you through such places as Anchor Point, Deadman's Cove, Nameless Cove and Eddie's Cove. The payoff to your time and travel is fantastic. L'Anse aux Meadows is the place where the Vikings established the first European settlement in North America over 1000 years ago. Native people had occupied this land for thousands of years before the newcomers arrived. According to Norse legend, sailor Bjarni Herjolfsson was blown off course sailing from Iceland to Greenland in 986. When he finally made port in Greenland, he reported seeing three new 'lands', believed to be north and south Labrador and Newfoundland.

He and his crew were the first Europeans to see North America. About 15 years later, Norse explorer Leif Erickson finally set foot on this 'new land' that Herjolfsson had discovered. He and his 30-man crew set up a small community around the year 1000. No one knows for sure how long they stayed. After they left the earthen buildings of the small community decayed and nature reclaimed the land for a long, long time. In 1960, the remains of this camp were discovered; and now the reconstructions of three Norse buildings form the focal point of this UNESCO World Heritage Site. These sod houses give visitors a taste of what life must have been like for those hearty souls. As early as the 1920s, Newfoundland author W.A. Munn had suggested that the 'Vinland' referred to in Norse Sagas might well be L'Anse aux Meadows. He could well be right!

L'Anse aux Meadows Visitor Centre.

PEGGY'S COVE

Perhaps the most famous lighthouse in all of Canada is situated at Peggy's Cove on Nova Scotia's picturesque South Shore near Halifax. Perched on an outcropping of granite over 40 million years old, this famous beacon is no longer operational in its lifesaving role for mariners, but the lighthouse continues its government service during the summer months as a post office, complete with its own cancellation stamp. Naturally, the stamp is a lighthouse.

The fishing village of Peggy's Cove is part of the much larger and equally scenic St. Margaret's Bay, and likely got its name because "Peggy" is a common nickname for Margaret. The more romantic version has the village named after the sole survivor of a 19th century shipwreck, washed up on the rocks during a hurricane. Legend has it that the young Peggy married a local and lived happily ever after.

For obvious reasons, the area is a summer Mecca for artists and photographers. Its stunning sunsets and friendly local flavour only add to the many reasons to visit. The very name Peggy's Cove is synonymous with the natural, unspoiled beauty of the south shore of Nova Scotia.

Peggy's Cove lighthouse.

NOVA SCOTIA

Three views of Peggy's Cove.

Swissair Flight 111 Memorial, Peggy's Cove.

The image and aura surrounding Peggy's Cove was forever changed on that terrible night of September 2nd, 1998 when, just a few kilometres off shore, Swissair Flight 111 was lost. Fishermen from the cove were among the first to join the search for survivors. In the years since the accident, families of the victims and residents of Peggy's Cove have developed strong personal bonds and friendships. Many residents continue to open their homes to families who visit the area each September to remember lost family members and spend time at the shoreline in quiet reflection.

Inscription on the memorial to Swissair Flight 111:

**In memory of
the 229 men, women and children
aboard Swissair Flight 111
who perished off these shores
September 2nd, 1998.
They have been joined to the sea, and the sky.
May they rest in peace.**

The flags of Switzerland and Nova Scotia fly in fitting tribute to the passengers and crew who perished, and reflect the personal bonds that developed following the crash. The setting is Shaw's Landing, a seafood restaurant in nearby West Dover.

Busking sisters provide a charming accompaniment to the setting sun on a lovely summer evening at Peggy's Cove.

In the midst of taking photographs of this lovely sunset, with charming fiddle music providing an almost unbearably perfect accompaniment to this magic moment, I became aware of a young woman talking quietly on her cell phone. Initially my reaction was negative. How could anyone talk on the phone at such a moment? But when her soft-spoken words reached me, my feelings quickly changed. She was sitting on a rock, off by herself, talking to her mother. And—that's right—she was describing how moved she was by the beauty of the moment as that sun slipped gently behind the far shore of St. Margaret's Bay.

Someone once wrote; "There is no joy in anything unshared." Part of the human condition is the need to share the experiences and events of our lives that touch us and, being alone, this was how she chose to respond to that need. I suppose this explains why most travel packages are based on double occupancy.

John McQuarrie

BLUENOSE II

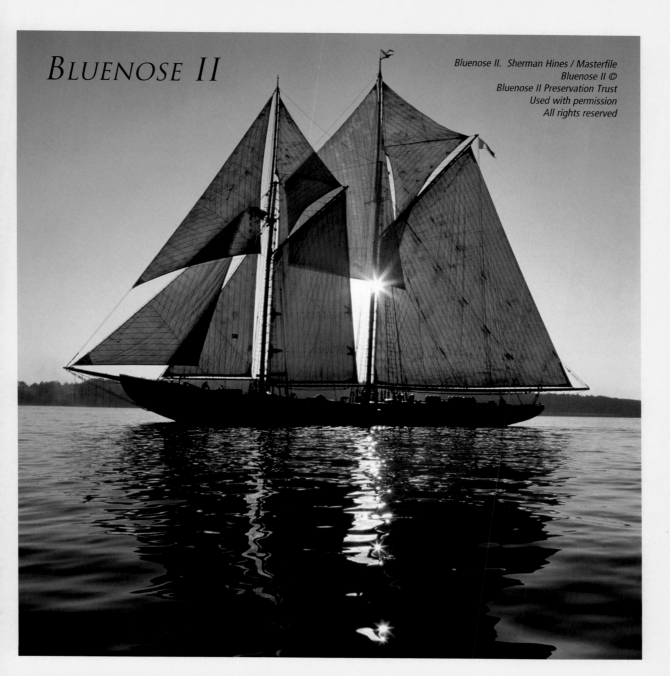

Since 1937, the schooner *Bluenose* has graced the back of the Canadian dime. The original *Bluenose* was a fishing vessel that doubled as the world's fastest ship on the water. She took on American challengers in the International Fishermen's Trophy races, and from 1921 to the final race in 1938, she was never beaten. Eventually sold to carry freight in the Caribbean, the *Bluenose* was lost on a Haitian reef in January of 1946. But rebirth occurred in a shipyard in Lunenburg early in the 1960's. Using the identical plans, and some of the same shipbuilders that worked on the original *Bluenose, Bluenose II* picked up the torch when she was launched in July of 1963. Owned by the Province, *Bluenose II* spends her summers in the waters off Atlantic Canada, ready to take you on the sail of a lifetime!

bluenose.novascotia.ca

Bluenose II under sail. Bluenose II, © Bluenose II Preservation Trust

Lunenburg harbour.

LUNENBURG

One of Nova Scotia's most picturesque and historic towns is Lunenburg on the province's South Shore. History drips from the town of 2,600 which was designated a UNESCO World Heritage Site in 1995 to recognize it as an outstanding example of a planned European colonial settlement. The area was first settled by French, German and Swiss immigrants in 1753, and some of the oldest churches in the country, built by those settlers, still stand.

Lunenburg is one of the best fishing ports in North America but, despite all its history, the town's chief claim to fame remains the honour of being the birthplace of Canada's legendary racing schooner, *Bluenose*, and her replica, *Bluenose II.*

The Fisheries Museum of the Atlantic, complete with five waterfront buildings and two historic ships, stands as a testament to maritime life in Atlantic Canada. Lunenburg is one of many jewels along the province's *Lighthouse Route* which hugs the breathtaking south shore of Nova Scotia.

Fishing boats and docks at Blue Rocks, southeast of Lunenburg.

MAGIC LOBSTER

This is not really a recipe. More like a Canadian ritual. And if you follow it precisely, the experience will remain with you longer than most.

Preparation Time: Your life until this moment
Cooking Time: 0
Ingredients:
2 market lobsters, cooked
1 bottle Nova Scotia white wine
1 medium sized rock (about 2 lbs)
1 corkscrew
No butter
No garlic
No salt or pepper

Ideally, you will be on a journey through the Maritimes when a roadside sign beckons: "Cooked Lobsters". Packed in ice – along with your wine – they will travel nicely for several hours as you search out your private dining place by the sea. Take the first side road where the sign includes the word "wharf". Best time is early evening, your pier quiet, atmosphere just right. Set yourself down on the edge of the dock, lobsters, rock and wine at hand. Gently tap the claws with said rock until they crack and *voila*, your meal is served. Tail and body can be opened with your hands so no utensils are required. As you savour your simple meal from the sea, by the sea, toss the scraps into the ocean where they will not go unappreciated.

Then let your mind wander, enjoying the lovely places it takes you.

HALIFAX

Aerial view of downtown Halifax with the Historic Properties–Privateers Wharf spread out before you along the waterfront.

It's not hard to see why this settlement became an important naval base as far back as the mid-1700s. Halifax harbour, which extends 26 kilometres inland from the Atlantic Ocean, offered unlimited natural protection to the Royal Navy and in later years, the Royal Canadian Navy. While Canada's eastern Navy still calls the city home, today's Halifax features a wonderful marriage of the recently restored Historic Properties-Privateer's Wharf area along the harbour and the more contemporary architecture that overlooks it all.

A centrepiece of the harbour, the Maritime Museum of the Atlantic commemorates the city's vital link with the sea and seafaring life through its displays of over 20,000 maritime artifacts. On my first visit to the museum I made a beeline up the stairs straight to the Titanic exhibit. It's here you'll find an original deck chair from the ill-fated ocean liner and the story of the Halifax connection to the disaster. Close by you'll find artifacts from the devastating Halifax explosion of 1917, when the Belgium relief ship *Imo* collided with the French munitions ship the *Mont Blanc*.

Night is descending on the Halifax skyline.

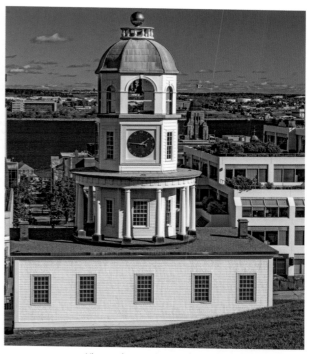

View to the east down Carmichael and George Streets, from the Citadel above the landmark Clock Tower.

The star-shaped Citidel occupies the high ground.

The *CSS Acadia*, Canada's first Hydrographic vessel and *HMCS Sackville*, the last of the World War II convoy escort Corvettes draw thousands of visitors every year. Canada's Naval Memorial, *Sackville* is maintained and operated by the Canadian Naval Memorial Trust, a non-profit society.

Great cities the world over often owe their location to early military considerations. While admirals looked to safe harbours, generals sought out hilltops. Halifax offered both.

Located on a hill overlooking downtown Halifax, the star shaped Citadel took 28 years to complete. Its purpose was to protect the city from a land-based attack that never came and it remains in pristine condition to this day as a national historic site. The massive green space around the fort that would once have discouraged any invader is enjoyed today as a scene for more peaceful pursuits, from picnics to outdoor concerts.

Halifax is fortunate that it has any history at all. In 1917, The French munitions ship *Mont Blanc* collided with the steamer *Imo*, and caught fire. The resulting explosion levelled the north end of the city, leaving 2,000 dead and many thousands more homeless. But somehow most of the historic buildings survived. One of the great beauties of the city is the compactness of its downtown. A stroll along the living history of the harbourside boardwalk and up to the Citadel, requires a walk of just a few blocks.

Dartmouth ferry enroute to Halifax.

Cape Breton's Margaree River Valley, (left and above) enveloped in an early morning mist, is a mecca for fly fisherman from around the world.

Aerial view of Fortress Louisbourg National Historic Site.

Dauphin Gate and interior view of Fortress Louisbourg.

Step back in time to 1744! Experience Louisbourg, a thriving seaport and capital of île Royale, today known as Cape Breton Island. During the height of the French regime, the Fortress was the third busiest port on the continent and one of France's key economic and military centres in the New World.

The settlement had a population of about 3200, 700 of whom were soldiers. Hugging the shore of the Atlantic Ocean, Louisbourg must have been a lively place, with its mix of Bretons, Normans, Basques, Germans, Swiss, Irish and the occasional Mi'kmaq Indian visitor. For most, the big attraction was the abundant supply of cod that brought great wealth to the colony. But alas, nothing lasts forever.

France and Britain declared war in 1744; and the next year, attacking the fortress from the rear, the British captured the area after a six-week siege. In 1749, the French regained Louisbourg through a treaty and improved its fortification. But in 1758, again attacking from the rear, a massive British force of 30,000 reclaimed the fortress. In 1760, the British blew up the fort and in 1768 they withdrew from Louisbourg, as its strategic position was no longer significant.

The site was ignored for two centuries, until 1961, when the federal government decided to reconstruct one fifth of the original settlement. Today the site is alive and well once again. Since only 20% was rebuilt, you can clearly see the remains of the other parts of the fortress, despite the overgrowth that has formed with time. In many ways, looking at what once was is as interesting as experiencing the restoration. The site remains a massive archaeological time capsule which stands today as North America's largest historical reconstruction.

Talcum powder sand of Black Brook Beach north of Ingonish. Visitors to Ingonish should plan on driving to this spot with a thermos of coffee in the pre-dawn darkness to savour a sunrise that will more than justify leaving your cozy motel room in the dark.

The natural beauty of Cape Breton is the backdrop for Louisbourg. The mingling of Gaelic culture with Acadian French and Mi'kmaq has created an island of Old World charm. Its wealth of coastal vistas, wilderness trails, glorious beaches and pastoral vignettes make it one of the most intriguing vacation spots in North America.

After visiting this part of Canada many times and interacting with the locals, I truly believe each and every person born in Cape Breton was blessed with the ability to either sing, to play an instrument, (most likely the fiddle!) or to dance! You can also insert any combination of the above for a lot of folks! To look around the island, at the highlands, the rivers, the coast, the beaches or the faces of the elders, is to look at the inspiration of these singers, songwriters, poets, musicians and dancers. They've been at it for hundreds of years, and there are still hundreds of years of inspiration left in the landscape.

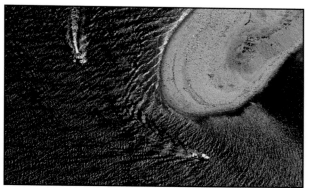

Aerial and ground views of Ingonish lobster boats.

Cabot Trail winding its way south along the western shore of Cape Breton Highlands National Park, just a few kilometres north of the Acadian town of Cheticamp.

Cape Smokey on the Cabot Trail, just south of the lovely seaside village of Ingonish.

You only *think* you're in the Scottish Highlands! Nova Scotia's Cabot Trail, in the Cape Breton Highlands is as breathtaking a drive as you'll ever make, and is considered one of North America's top scenic marine drives. The loop that makes up the trail, takes you right through Cape Breton Highlands National Park. Here you can stop for a short hike to the rocky edge of the ocean or linger for a day hike on one of the park's many trails. There are country inns and bed and breakfasts everywhere, and charming little villages like Ingonish, Margaree Harbour and Chéticamp. You could drive the entire trail in half a day, but don't! Take your time. In fact, drive it in both directions. The villages and towns won't change, but the view surely will.

Cap Rouge showing her stormy side. Sherman Hines / Masterfile

The highest tides in the world, twice a day, every day, are seen in the Bay of Fundy, the body of water separating the provinces of New Brunswick and Nova Scotia. At their highest, with the gravitational pull of a full moon, the tides rise and fall some 14 to 16 metres at the eastern end of the Bay of Fundy, in the Minas Basin of Nova Scotia (photo above) and Chignecto Bay in New Brunswick. This phenomenon occurs because the Bay of Fundy is relatively shallow and narrow and the ebb and flow of the ocean tide pushes water in and out in a span of only 12 hours. Tides at the mouth are five metres and go up as you head into the ever-narrowing bay.

With water constantly moving and churning up the bottom, humpback, fin, minke and right whales have come here to feed every summer for thousands of years. Shorebirds and sea life flourish.

Moncton looking to the north over the muddy bottom of the Petitcodiac River.

Even though Moncton is more than 50 kilometres up the Petitcodiac River from the Bay of Fundy, its famous tidal bore causes the river level to jump 7.5 metres in less than an hour as the tide waters surge over the mud flats.

Low tide in Minas Basin, Five Islands Provincial Park, Nova Scotia. Daryl Benson / Masterfile
Aerial view of Flowerpot Rocks at low tide and high tide view from observation deck of the Hopewell Rocks Ocean Tidal Exploration Site.

At the sandstone flowerpot formations of New Brunswick's Hopewell Rocks, you can walk on the ocean floor, then return later to see your footsteps washed away by the incoming high tide. It's a real experience to explore the seabed on foot in the morning, then sea kayak over the very same area in the afternoon, with the water now some 10 to 14 metres higher.

SAINT JOHN

Saint John from the Fort Howe Lookout, site of an English fort built in 1778. Greg Stott / Masterfile

Visitor Centre at Reversing Falls. In this view the incoming tide is causing the river to run upstream while, in the aerial view below, the flow is downstream during low tide.

Discovered on St. Jean Baptiste day in 1604 by Samuel de Champlain and named accordingly, Saint John became the first incorporated city in Canada in 1785.

Home to one of the busiest and deepest ports in Atlantic Canada, it has oil terminals serving some of the largest ships in the world. Tides in the harbour rise and fall some five metres so you could be sitting in one of the cozy waterfront restaurants watching as ships disappear or reappear with the tides. Waterfront redevelopment has brought this part of the city back to life as old warehouses have been transformed into shops, boutiques and restaurants.

The famous Reversing Falls might be a bit of a misnomer but it is impressive and certainly worth a look. The spectacular water show is created where the Saint John River flows into the Bay of Fundy. At low tide, the river falls some 16 metres into the bay. Then, as the tide rises, there is a period of slack when the water in the river and the water in the bay reach an equal level. But that lasts less than half an hour before high tide begins to push the mighty Saint John River into reverse. The tide rises another four metres creating swiftly moving rapids that now flow upstream, hence the name.

Saint John is also a city of great walks. Self-guided tours take you downtown in the footsteps of the city's Loyalist founders and through Edwardian commercial and residential areas. Like much of Atlantic Canada, the city gets more than its fair share of fog in the summer, but you just can't beat an evening stroll in light rain and mist as you meander through the city's history.

Carleton Martello Tower National Historic Site offers a spectacular view of Saint John.

Both the Fort Howe Lookout and Carleton Martello Tower offer great views of the city along with a glimpse into the past. The Tower is a national historic site; its familiar, circular profile visible from most parts of the city. Completed in 1815, it served in defence of Saint John Habour until 1944.

No visit to Saint John is complete until you've wandered through the historic City Market. This is the oldest continuing farmers market in Canada, serving the community since 1876. When you walk into the building, look up! The signature feature of the market is its roof, an architectural wonder. The system of rafters were built from hand-hewn timbers and assembled in the same manner as a ship's hull, albeit upside down. And don't forget to try the dulse when you're there. Many New Brunswickers consider this dried out seaweed a delicacy. I had a little different reaction, but you be the judge!

Restaurants lining the west side of Loyalist Plaza.

Interior view of the Saint John City Market.

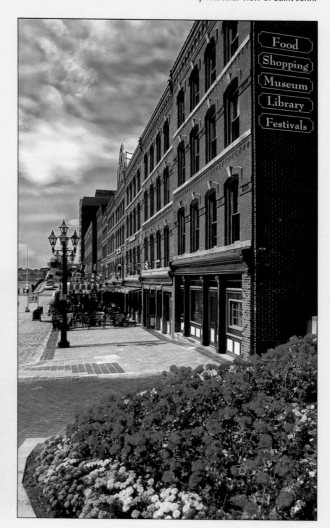

Morning light near Jemseg. Freeman Patterson / Masterfile

There is something—call it a feeling—about the Maritimes that is hard to put into words. There's a feel and texture to the place that you just don't encounter anywhere else. When you visit, you sense it: the warmth of the people, the warmth of the light of day, the warmth of a sunset, and knowing how to savour what nature provides. It's a place you can take the time to walk through natural and human history. A place where you can be a million miles from home yet feel like you *are* home. A place to listen to dancing fiddles, thumping feet, strumming guitars and rich voices that echo out for no reason other than it feels good.

To make a living from the sea, but not take away from the sea. To protect what they have, yet at the same time share their land. To hear songs written from the heart about the pride of living in Atlantic Canada, where people play the cards they are dealt as if every hand were four of a kind. Canada's smallest province is here, and so are some of Canada's smallest cities. More people live in Winnipeg, Manitoba than in all of New Brunswick. The city of Kitchener, Ontario has more people than Prince Edward Island; and the population of Halifax proper, the largest city in Atlantic Canada, is just under 120 thousand. No one here thinks that's too small, and no one would wish it any other way.

Morning light, Kingston. Freeman Patterson / Masterfile

A rising sun silhouettes the boardwalk of 'La dune de Bouctouche' at the Irving Eco-Centre just north of the town of Bouctouche.

One of the many unique attractions that dot the east coast of New Brunswick is the Irving Eco-Centre at La dune de Bouctouche. The white sand dune that stretches 12 kilometres across Bouctouche Bay is a result of the constant action of wind, tides and sea currents since the last ice age. After every major storm its shape changes. This environmentally significant area is the habitat for a rich variety of marine and aquatic plants and animals and for shorebirds and migratory birds.

Created to celebrate the fictional characters of renowned novelist and playwright Antonine Maillet, le Pays de la Sagouine (left) is an island of legends, music and theatre celebrating the rich Acadian history in the Bouctouche area.

La Pays de la Sangouine, Bouctouche.
Entrance to the two kilometre long boardwalk of the Irving Eco-Centre.

The Algonquin, a renowned Canadian Pacific Hotel, now part of the Fairmont chain, is St. Andrews' dominant landmark.

Water Street, St. Andrews-by-the-Sea.

Canada's oldest seaside resort town is the delightful St. Andrews-by-the-Sea, tucked into the southeast corner of the province. The signature landmark is the Fairmont Algonquin Hotel. Built in 1889, it overlooks not only the village but also picturesque Passamaquoddy Bay. And it may or may not be true that room 473 of this hotel is haunted, but certainly search out one of the town's ghost story tellers and find out if it's true! The town was founded in 1783 by United Empire Loyalists who chose to remain loyal to the British Crown following the American Revolution. Many crossed the bay to their new country with all their worldly possessions including – for some – their homes, which they dismantled and rebuilt here. Some are still standing today. Over 250 buildings in downtown St. Andrews are between 100 and 200 years old.

Fredericton is the capital of New Brunswick. Located on a bend on the scenic Saint John River, it's one of the oldest settlements in North America. It was first inhabited by Maliseet Indians thousands of years ago. As in St. Andrews-By-the-Sea, United Empire Loyalists also settled here in 1783 and it's been the provincial capital since 1785. The Old Government House and Historic Garrison District have been named both provincial and national historic sites. The city is renowned for its architecture, culture and heritage.

Fredericton's City Hall.

Officers' Quarters, Fredericton.

Christ Church Cathedral.

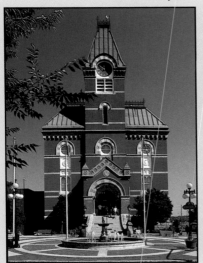

Just west of the provincial capital of Fredericton you'll find King's Landing Historical Settlement. Located in the Saint John River valley, it's a place to step back in time in a recreation of an historical settlement spanning the years from the 1800s. Here you will find more than 70 buildings, including a grist mill, old English pub, historic homes, print shop, school, church and a wheelwright's shop. More than 100 costumed guides are there to help you make your way through the village and its 70,000 artifacts. You could ask the wheelwright to make a new wheel for your wagon! In 1968, an 80-kilometre section of the Saint John River valley was flooded with the opening of the Mactaquac Dam. Most of the buildings at King's Landing were rescued from this area and preserved to give a living, breathing glimpse of life in New Brunswick in the 19th century.

Aerial view of King's Landing.

Bill Brooks / Masterfile

J. A. Kraulis / Masterfile

At 391 metres, or 1,282 feet, the longest covered bridge in the world spans the Saint John River at Hartland, New Brunswick. Built in 1901, the bridge went uncovered for some 20 years. After ice destroyed two spans in 1920, the bridge was covered two years later to increase the life of the span. Many refer to covered bridges as "kissing" bridges, and certainly all 900 people who live in Hartland could easily be accommodated in this one for a smooch or two! Some historians suggest the term originated because the covered bridge offered couples an ideal spot for privacy and darkness at night, before returning to the residential streets of the city. One can only imagine how many horses "ran out of gas" in the middle of the great Hartland Bridge!

Bridges weren't covered for romantic or aesthetic reasons; but rather, for practical ones. Uncovered bridges of the era began to fall apart after 10 years due to the elements—sun, ice, snow, and rain. Covered bridges, on the other hand, were expected to last for at least 80 years or longer, as the Hartland Bridge has proven. Another reason to cover a bridge was to calm horses which could easily be spooked by the rushing water below. The covered bridge offers the comforting atmosphere of a barn.

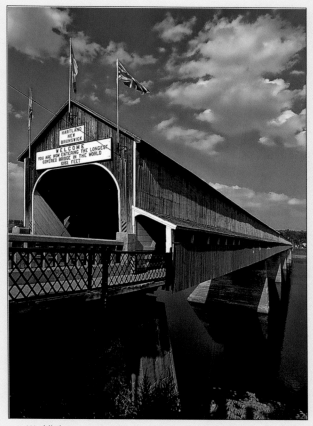

World's longest covered bridge crosses the Saint John River at Hartland.

Kingston Creek. Freeman Patterson / Masterfile

PRINCE EDWARD ISLAND

Fishing boat departing Naufrage Harbour.

Aerial and beach-level views of the Confederation Bridge.

CONFEDERATION BRIDGE

Taking a ferry to get on—or off—Prince Edward Island was a way of life for hundreds of years. But that all changed in 1997 when the Confederation Bridge, linking PEI to New Brunswick, officially opened. Crossing the Northumberland Strait is now a 10-minute drive over the 12.9 kilometre span, as opposed to long line-ups for an hourly ferry that was weather-dependent and always busy. The highest point on the bridge is 60 metres above the water while the average height is 40 metres but despite extreme high winds that regularly plague the strait, its robust construction has meant the bridge has only rarely been forced to close.

The bridge has a hollow core that acts as a utility corridor for electrical, telephone and other services to the Island. PEI, with no train tracks since 1989, now has goods transported to the island in minutes. The real winner has been tourism. People are flocking to PEI in record numbers to enjoy the world famous seafood, beaches and historic sites. They can also bike and play a few rounds on the island's ever-expanding array of golf courses. When travelling over the bridge, be sure to look for the bridge construction "grave yard" on the right as you enter PEI. Many concrete remnants and bridge forms are lined up in eerie fashion, a la Stonehenge – an isolated ode to a remarkable engineering challenge and achievement.

Even with an influx of tourists, a deserted beach is easier to find than a crowded one on PEI. Since you're never more than 20 minutes from the water, getting to the shore is no problem! From the world famous beach at Cavendish, to the signature dunes at Basin Head, to the sheer expanse of Prince Edward Island National Park, there's a beach to suit all those looking to pack their worries away for an hour, a day or a season. Sands of white, pink, red and champagne greet you at the seashore as yet another lonely lighthouse evokes thoughts of mariners past. Family outings seem to come alive when the kids' bare feet first hit the talcum powder smooth sand.

Here they can run and laugh to their hearts' delight with no worries that a tumble in the soft sand will be a problem – just a burst of more spirited laughter. No matter how loud their shrieks of delight, the wind will carry them away with only the occasional seagull complaining. And all this exercise, combined with great gulps of fresh, salt-laced air will guarantee the kids a sound sleep; allowing the parents to sneak out in the pre-dawn darkness the next morning for a sunrise stroll amidst gently rolling waves lapping up on shore. Same beach but with an entirely different feeling at this magical hour!

Beach and dunes at the O'Sullivan Estate, Lakeside.

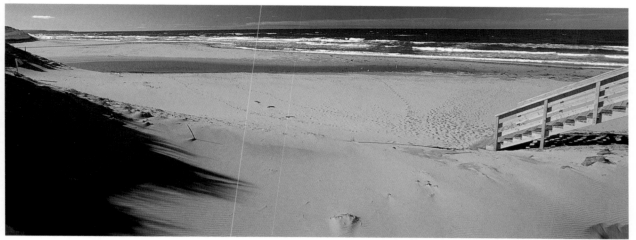

Talcum powder beach typical of Prince Edward Island National Park.

Dunes and characteristic red sand of Prince Edward Island National Park.

Covehead Lighthouse, Prince Edward Island National Park.

Farmhouse at Green Gables.

ANNE OF GREEN GABLES

Let's play a word association game. When I say Prince Edward Island, you say...? Well, if you're like millions across Canada and around the world, your answer is Anne of Green Gables. PEI author Lucy Maud Montgomery wrote *Anne of Green Gables* and 22 other books starring the orphaned red-haired, pigtailed heroine Anne. The books were about Anne's life and times in and around the fictional PEI village of Avonlea. While Avonlea exists only on the page and in the hearts and minds of readers worldwide, Lucy Maud Montgomery based it on the small north shore town she grew up in: picturesque Cavendish.

"Cavendish is, to a large extent, Avonlea. Green Gables was drawn from David MacNeil's house, though not so much the house itself as the situation and scenery, and the truth of my description of it is attested by the fact that everyone has recognized it"
L.M. Montgomery, *The Selected Journals of L.M. Montgomery*, Vol. II, Friday January 27, 1911.

Birth place of Lucy Maude Montgomery, author of Anne of Green Gables.

Today, visitors from around the world flock to Cavendish for the Avonlea experience and to visit the homestead, which has been restored to portray the Victorian period setting in which Mongomery grew up. In 1943, Montgomery was recognized by Canada as being a person of national historicial significance. Just outside Cavendish, in New London, the birthplace of Lucy Maud Montgomery is open to the public. It's still in great condition, and stands ordinarily at the junction of two roads, in a village with just a few other houses.

Just outside the village you'll find jaw-dropping seascapes featuring PEI's famous red sandstone cliffs and the entrance to Prince Edward Island National Park which, like Cavendish, lies on the Gulf of St. Lawrence, part of the Atlantic Ocean. A favourite of hikers and bikers, the park features, beaches, stunning red cliffs, sweeping wind blown sand dunes, salt marshes and woodlands.

Aerial view of Green Gables.

One of the aspects of travel that remains with us longer than most is a particularly memorable view, one that you know at the time will go into that special drawer in the backroom of your mind. The stillness and surreal beauty of this twilight vista of North Rustico Harbour made my lobster supper, taken on the far end of the pier pictured at right, all the more enjoyable. And the shoreline of Prince Edward Island National Park can be counted upon to dish up sunsets, as in the inset photo at left, with remarkable regularity.

CHARLOTTETOWN

In 1864, the Fathers of Confederation met at Province House in Charlottetown to discuss the politics and economics of founding a nation. Three years later, in 1867, as a result of those meetings, the Dominion of Canada was born. Ironically, the "Cradle of Confederation did not join Canada untill 1873. Province House still stands proudly at the head of historic, and now restored, Great George Street and to this day, continues to house the PEI provincial legislature. With a population of less than 40 thousand, Charlottetown is Canada's smallest capital, although arguably the one with the most charm. Old warehouse areas like Victoria Row are now flourishing with restaurants, taverns, shops and boutiques.

Charlottetown waterfront and Confederation Landing.

Province House.

Built to commemorate the birth of Canada, Confederation Landing is a collection of marinas, restaurants and parkland.

Everything here is within walking distance and you can start your tour with a stroll up Great George Street to historic Province House. In doing this, you will be following in the footsteps of the Fathers of Confederation who, upon arriving at the docks, walked this same route to their meeting with destiny. On your way, notice the wonderful old buildings on either side of the street. Many of them were in place on that momentous day back in 1864.

Cafés and shops of Victoria Row.

Potato fields near Sea View. Gary Black / Masterfile

The signature landscape of Prince Edward Island is its gently rolling fields and iron-rich red soil, a combination allowing PEI to harvest some of the best potatoes in the world. Farming, fishing and tourism are the island's three main industries and. as you can see by this spread, PEI is also a photographer's delight.

The island is 224 kilometres long and anywhere from six to 64 kilometres wide. Water is never far away. Red soil is everywhere. It's not hard to get lost in the beauty of it all. Charm oozes from every nook and cranny of the island, dotted with picturesque farms, church steeples and quaint shops. At water's edge are to be found some of the world's best mussels and oysters and, in places like New Glasgow, North Rustico, and St. Ann, busloads of tourists come for world-famous lobster suppers.

Rich red soil furrowed and ready for planting potato crop, Springbrook.
Dale Wilson / Masterfile

Potato crop several weeks into the growing season, Springbrook.
Gary Black / Masterfile

Barn and tractor near Glenwood. Daryl Benson / Masterfile

From Tignish in the west, to Elmira in the east, the Confederation Trail is a haven for bikers and hikers throughout the summer. Once bustling with noisy train traffic the trail, with tracks removed, is a serene adventure taking you truly off the beaten path—throughout the length and breadth of the island—to see places once reserved for brakemen and engineers.

Bales of hay in rolling field near Brookfield.

Sunrise in fog silhouettes house and barn near Brookfield.

Aerial view of Cape Tryon Llighthouse.

North Head Lighthouse.

Panmure Island Lighthouse.

West Head Lighthouse.

Panmure Island Lighthouse.

QUEBEC

Canoeist paddling through a circle of Fall colour on Meech Lake.

The two photographs on these pages show a section of the Gatineau River near Ottawa in fall and winter.

This spread to me is typical of the beauty of Canada. In both pictures you're looking at the Gatineau River near Ironsides Quebec, close to the nation's capital. The beauty of the winter shot is only matched by the beauty of a shot from the same location taken in the autumn. It's almost impossible to pick a favourite! These waters, like many in and around the Ottawa region, are filled with both the natural beauty of all four seasons, and the rich history of those who first settled the land.

While these waters were used mainly as commercial arteries for centuries, tourists have replaced the voyageurs as the explorers of today. Discovering these rivers will give you an idea of how those early explorers must have felt when they first came upon the magnificent beauty of the area. Until recently, the river was also the scene of massive log drives every spring. The big bonus is that the landscape and rivers, for the most part, remain the same today as they did centuries ago.

Gaspé's famous Percé Rock as seen from the air and at sea level.
(left) Daryl Benson / Masterfile   (above)

Isolated, unspoiled, and for the most part, undiscovered, one of Canada's most scenic areas is the Gulf of St. Lawrence region. The Gaspé area is associated with the very beginnings of the country of Canada and the modern history of North America. The cross that the explorer Jacques Cartier erected here in 1534, earned Gaspé the title of the cradle of Canada. But undoubtedly, it is most famous for Percé Rock. Every Canadian school kid learns about it, but most have only seen the landmark in pictures. At low tide you can walk out to this giant that measures 1500 feet in length, 270 feet in width, and rises a stunning 275 feet out of the water. Its fivemillion tons of calcium contain fossils that are up to 400 million years old.

Sea kayakers enjoying Saguenay Fjord.
J. F. Bergeron/Parks Canada/05.53.07.19.37

Marteau Island, Mingan Archipelago National Park Reserve.
Pierre St-Jacques/Parks Canada/05.52.07.04.01

The Mingan Archipelago National Park Reserve, some 800 kilometres northeast of Quebec City, extends for nearly 175 kilometres along the north shore of the St. Lawrence, opposite Anticosti Island. The Reserve is a beautiful scattering of 40 islands and more than 2000 reefs and islets. It's a remarkable environment, carved out of limestone bedrock which bears witness to the never-ending wear of the sea and the centuries.

The Saguenay fjord (left) is the main component of the Saguenay-St. Lawrence Marine Park. A playground for fin and beluga whales in the late spring and summer, the fjord features dramatic rock canyons up to two kilometres wide as it stretches 100 kilometres from the mouth at Tadoussac to the source at Saint-Fulgence near Chicoutimi. There are times in the summer here where you can literally pull up a lawn chair at the fjord's edge, and watch whales frolic just a few hundred yards away.

Summer and winter views of Montmorency Falls. At 83 metres, these falls are a full 30 metres higher than those of Niagara.

QUEBEC CITY

Few cities in the New World can boast of more history than Quebec City, known as the cradle of French civilization on the continent, and the "Gibraltar of America". When explorer Samuel de Champlain came upon the site on the St. Lawrence River in 1608, he immediately recognized the potential of the location and quickly set up a trading post. Quebec City was born.

As a French colony, the city prospered in the 1600's but history changed in 1759. After a naval siege, the British scaled the cliffs east of the city, taking the French forces by surprise. In the 20-minute battle that ensued French General Montcalm's forces were defeated by General Wolfe, although both men died of wounds sustained in the fighting. National Battlefield Park now occupies this historic site on the Plains of Abraham.

Summer and winter views of Quebec City harbour dominated by the grand Chateau Frontenac Hotel.

There is more to Quebec City than the impressive old city. As the capital of the province of Quebec, the National Legislative Assembly meets in a parliament building well over 125 years old. The city is a centre of commerce, research and politics and, of course, one of the cultural hotspots of Canada. The population here is predominantly French-speaking and has been so since Champlain first set foot on the land early in the 17th century and French settlement began.

Chateau Frontenac Hotel and boardwalk overlooking the Old City

Today, Quebec City remains profoundly French. Its old Lower and Upper Towns are still separated by walls built almost 400 years ago. The walls extend for nearly five kilometres and are three to four metres thick. A walk through the old part of Quebec is a walk back in time. The original, winding, narrow streets and old residential, military and religious buildings with thick walls and small rooms still stand. The walls were refortified by the British in the 1800's to defend against a threat of American invasion.

Perched atop Cap Diamant, the Citadel is the largest fortification in North America still occupied by regular troops.

Dating from 1608, the magnificently restored Place Royale is the birthplace of French civilization in North America.

It was at Place Royale that Samuel de Champlain began construction of his fortified *abitation* or trading post when he founded Quebec City in 1608. Built at the foot of Cap Diamant, it became the first permanent establishment in New France.

Today the area has been meticulously restored to its 17th century splendour, helping to win Quebec City a place on UNESCO's list of World Heritage Sites. The claim that it is the oldest shopping district in North America is difficult to argue after you have explored its myriad of narrow and enchanting streets and alleyways.

L'église Notre-Dame-des Victoires is the centrepiece of Place Royale. Built in 1688, it is the oldest church in North America.

Place des Livernois in the Latin Quarter (above), mansard roofs surrounding Place Royale (right) and the Auberge du Trésor on Place d' Armes (below right).

Impressive from the ground or the air, Quebec City's Citadel (top left) was built by the British between 1820 and 1852 to solidify their defence systems in North America. The Citadel remains the largest fortification still garrisoned by regular troops in North America and is one of two official residences for the Governor General of Canada. It's home to the famous Royal 22nd Regiment, popularly known as the "Van Doos" and in the summer the public can witness the regiment staging various military ceremonies, including the ever-popular Changing of the Guard on the large parade square. Strategically located overlooking the St. Lawrence River, the fortress was built on the site of former French defences.

Romance and mystery abound in old Quebec, and no place has more of it than does the Auberge du Trésor (bottom right) on Place d'Armes, opposite the grand old Chateau Frontenac. Opened in 1679, the little auberge is said to have been the scene of the first French kiss on this continent. It is also believed to have been built over the grave of Samuel de Champlain, the explorer who founded the city back in 1608.

Gare du Palais (train and bus station), a building in the Chateau style popularized by the Canadian Pacific Railway in their grand hotels of the early 20th century.

View to the northeast from the observation deck on the 31st floor of the Marie-Guyart Building. Île-d'Orléans can be seen on the horizon where it splits the St. Lawrence River. A closer look will reveal people enjoying the city's renowned "Carnaval".

For a minority of Canadians, the only good thing about winter is the added joy it brings to the month of May. But a true "Canuck" savours the change of seasons; and when the last red maple leaf hits the ground, realizes it is time to move the garden tools, roller blades and golf clubs into that spot in the garage where the snow shovel and skis spent the summer.

Of all Canadian cities, Quebec does winter best. And the centrepiece of it all has, for over half a century, been the Quebec Winter Carnival. For three weeks in February *Carnaval* attracts almost 1,000,000 visitors who watch and participate in every form of winter activity imaginable. Ice and snow sculpture, skating, dog-sledding, cross-country skiing, tobogganing, winter camping, horse-drawn calèche rides and a myriad of related events offer something for everyone.

Du Petit-Champlain Street, running along the base of the cliff upon which the Chateau Frontenac is perched, offers a European ambiance with its wealth of craft shops and artisans.

Maison Fradet, a charming Bed & Breakfast on L'île-d'Orléans built in 1830.

The Jacquet House, built in 1674, is the oldest home in Quebec City. Today it is home to the restaurant Aux Anciens Canadiens.

Canadians, out of necessity, must embrace the cold or remain indoors for the three to four months of winter. Here we see people taking advantage of snow and ice at the Carnaval and nearby ski hills.

Dog sledding and canoe races across the St. Lawrence River have been staple attractions of the Carnaval for decades.

As the ice begins to retreat from Canadian rivers and lakes in late winter, the longer days of approaching spring also signal the maple trees to start their flow of life-giving sap. Many of these trees are tapped and the harvested sap is boiled down to produce the sweet syrup the country is famous for. It takes from 30 to 40 litres of sap to produce a litre of syrup. Just as the red maple leaf has become a symbol of Canada, appearing in the centre of its flag, the sweet elixer produced from the tree has also become a Canadian icon. Canada produces 76% of the world's maple syrup. Many Canadians view an annual pilgrimage to the nearest maple sugar camp as a sure sign that the long winter is nearing its end.

A late winter snow storm is Mother Nature's way of showing Canadians that even if the ice on the Gatineau River at Wakefield, Quebec has begun to melt, she is still in charge of the seasons, despite what the calendar may be claiming.

Maple sugar camp evaporating sap down to syrup.
The Stewarts Maple Products, Mississippi Mills, Ontario., near Ottawa.

MONTREAL

A bustling market and meeting place at the turn of the 20th century, Place Jacques Cartier has become a signature street of Old Montreal. Take your calèche over century-old cobblestones on a tour of the Old City, stopping to browse the many shops, boutiques and restaurants in buildings that have stood the test of time. In the summer, Place Jacques Cartier comes alive with street performers, tourists, shoppers and café-goers in an area virtually unchanged since the late 1800's.

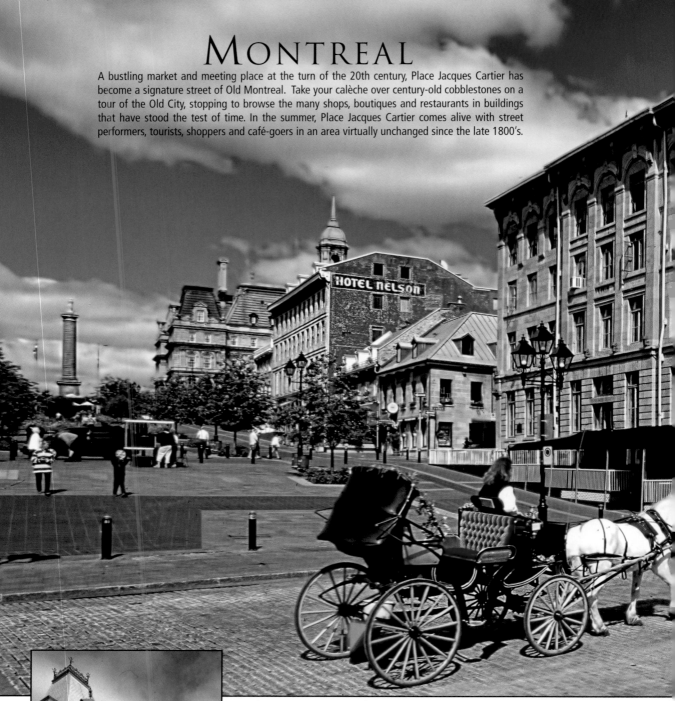

Place Jacques Cartier at rue de la Commune in Old Montreal.

While looking for a passageway to the Orient in 1535, off-course French explorer Jacques Cartier came upon an island in what is now the St. Lawrence River. The island had a mountain, which Cartier named Mount Royal, and an Iroquois village which he called "Hochelaga". Some 70 years later, Samuel de Champlain set up a furtrading post in the area. In 1642, under the leadership of Paul Chomedey de Maisonneuve, Ville-Marie was founded as a missionary outpost.

Today the city of Montreal stands as a testament to the past and present; a thriving bilingual, multicultural city, with the second largest French-speaking population in the world. While downtown Montreal thrives as a major commercial and business centre with modern office towers, you're never more than a stone's throw away from Victorian-era architecture, as Old Montreal is resplendent with historical churches, homes and commercial buildings from the 19th and early 20th century.

Colourful 19th century row homes line St. Louis Square.

Dining "alfresco" has a long tradition in Montreal and the outdoor cafés that abound in the Old Montreal area often invoke the flavour and feeling of Euruopean cities.

The soft, first light of sunrise illuminates this row of 19th century warehouses lining rue de la Commune.

Magnificent view to the south over McGill University Campus from atop Mount Royal.

Aerial view to the south over Beaver Lake in Mount Royal Park.

Lookout atop Mount Royal on a beautiful summer afternoon.

MOUNT ROYAL

People of Montreal have been escaping to Mount Royal since the 1870's to get away from it all and enjoy the spacious park at the top of the mountain. Tourists and photographers today go to Mount Royal to see it all. The panorama of the city and surrounding area has drawn people to this spot for hundreds of years. Downtown shot? It's there. City landscape shot? It's there. A view of the splendour of Mount Royal Park? It's there. Winter or summer, the view is magnificent, the vistas are stunning, and history unfolds before your eyes.

One of Montreal's star attractions, Mount Royal Park opened in the spring of 1876. With a surging population and increased industrialization with its accompanying pollution, Mayor Aldis Bernard wanted to create a green place in the city where citizens could relax in a healthy environment. The concept for the park on the mountain was born. Fredrick Law Olmsted, the landscape architect responsible for New York's Central Park, designed it. Olmsted preserved the natural beauty of the mountain in his design, which included a network of roads, paths and trails streaming down from the top of the mountain to open the forest to hikers, skiers and riders. The park is designed for all-season use. It's hard to believe as you nestle into one of the thousands of tranquil settings provided by the park, that just below you lies one of the world's most cosmopolitan cities.

Lookout atop Mount Royal on a beautiful winter afternoon.

Embarkation point for calèche tours in Mount Royal Park.

Aerial view of Place du Canada and Mary Queen of the World Cathedral.

Notre-Dame-de-Bonsecours Chapel in Old Montreal.

The pictures on these pages illustrate just how much Montrealers cherish the old and the new. The Mount Royal views at left give a sense of a modern metropolis looking to the future. Now look closely at the aerial view of the Dominion Square area above. Surrounded by contemporary office towers we see the lovingly respected Mary Queen of the World Cathedral. Completed in 1894, after 24 years of construction, the cathedral is a one-third-scale replica of St. Peter's in Rome. Then, in the photo at top right, we see tiny Notre-Dame-de-Bonsecours Chapel located in the heart of the Old Port, but just minutes from the downtown business heart of Dominion Square.

The city of Montreal hosted the world with Expo '67 in Canada's centennial year of 1967. St. Helen's Island was one of the islands that housed this celebration and today you can take a lazy walk on the site and see sculptures and the few buildings left over from the exposition. The island is also the site of the Olympic rowing basin from the 1976 Summer Olympics and home to Circuit Gilles Villeneuve, scene of annual Formula One and Indy-type car races. When it's not in use, you're free to don roller blades and skate around the track to your heart's content. Or maybe you can do a few laps on your bicycle, but if you hear a deafening roar, you may have picked the wrong day for your spin.

View of city skyline over fall colour of St. Helen's Island.

Place d'Armes square begining to fill with the lunch crowds.

View of Montreal Skyline from the Jacques Cartier Bridge at sunrise.

View of Montreal and her mountain from St. Helen's Island.

A golden shot of the skyline of the city of Montreal. Look closely at this image. Photography makes it look more compact than it really is, but it's not hard to see how this city was developed from the waterfront inland. Old Montreal has always been the heart and soul of the city. The oldest buildings were constructed near the water's edge as the commerce of early Montreal was dependent on the river. The silver dome of the Bonsecours market has watched over changing times for generations. Standing guard at the entrance to the Old Port is the tall white clock tower built in 1922 as a memorial to merchant seamen lost during the First World War

A little further back you see the late 19th, and early 20th century commercial buildings, the country's first skyscrapers, and they in turn are dwarfed by the skyscrapers of today. The Old Port of Montreal underwent a great renaissance towards the end of the 20th century. As times changed, so did the requirements of Montreal's waterfront. While it remains the world's largest inland port, the advent of the shipping container and larger container ships caused the port activity to move to new facilities at the east end of the island, leaving behind a blight of decaying industrial buildings that sealed the harbour off from pedestrians.

Aerial view of the Old Port and the downtown area.

Aerial view of the downtown core looking to the east.

Fortunately, most succumbed to the wrecker's ball or were transformed for new uses, and the Old Port is now an entertainment, cultural and recreational centre, complete with generous parks and gardens framed by walking, biking and roller blading paths. The city boasts hundreds of kilometres of trails that encompass, among other areas, the waterfront, Lachine Canal, summer outdoor markets and the islands of Notre Dame and St. Helen. These trails are laid out in such a way that those using them never have to cross a main street. Traffic in Montreal can be, to say the least… well, let's just leave it at busy…all the time!

Day or night, Montreal is the Canadian city that never sleeps. From the rollicking nightlife of the discotheques, jazz clubs, taverns and bars to the serenity of a peaceful walk through the city's majestic botanical gardens. A sightseeing tour of the Olympic Stadium or an escape to one of the four eco-systems displayed in the Biodome, Montreal is a city for all seasons.

Oh, by the way, what you've heard about the bagels and smoked meat in this city is true. Don't leave without trying them both!

THE ST. LAWRENCE

The St. Lawrence River begins its flow to the Atlantic from Ontario's Great Lakes. But early explorers like Jacques Cartier and Samuel de Champlain could sail no further upstream than what is now Montreal. The reason? The bubbling, churning, unforgiving waters of the Lachine Rapids. Many an early voyageur (and voyageur canoe) was lost to these waters just upstream from the city. European goods arriving by ship would be transferred to canoes and later on, to railcars for more westerly destinations. These ships would then return to Europe laden with Canada's first export: Furs. So the Lachine Rapids were responsible for the creation of this great city, and will forever also be known as the place where the poor little beaver first became a source for generating wealth.

In 1825 the Lachine Canal was completed, allowing ships to continue their journey up the St. Lawrence into Ontario and the Great Lakes. The canal remained in use until 1959, when the St. Lawrence Seaway opened, enabling larger, ocean going vessels of the times access to those Great Lakes ports. Ironically, history has repeated itself in that today's huge container ships have again outgrown the locks of the Seaway system, so Montreal is once again, an end point for goods arriving by ship.

Thrill seekers can challenge the famous Lachine Rapids on the jet boats of the Saute Mouton company. It's quite a ride. Despite the raincoats, passengers become one with the rapids literally; as what feels like the whole St. Lawrence River comes crashing into the boat, hitting you like a duffelbag full of sand. Next thing you know you're sitting knee deep in water which rushes out the back just in time for the next assault. When it's over, you're exhausted, soaked, exhilarated, and can hardly wait to do it again. And this white-water adventure is all taking place within sight of the city.

(Below) Day and night views of the skyline from the Habitat 67 condominum complex designed by architect Moshe Safdie for Expo 67.

Jet boat of the Saute Mouton company providing white water thrills in the Lachine Rapids, within sight of the city and her mountain.

Aerial view of Champlain Lookout in Quebec's Gatineau Park. This wildnerness park is located in the hills overlooking the Ottawa River and Canada's Capital.

With the coming of fall, Canadians are of two minds. We lament the passing of yet another warm and languid summer and begin to feel the exhilaration that the increasingly fresh mornings bring. Soon it will be winter, time for skating, skiing, snowboarding or tobogganing. Getting out to enjoy the breathtaking colour of the fall leaves is the perfect way to make the transition.

Gatineau Park is a superb nature reserve just 15 minutes from Parliament Hill in Ottawa. It serves as a reminder that protecting wilderness enclaves is a cherished Canadian value.

The Park is endowed with hundreds of kilometres of trails and forests containing more than forty species of trees, abundant wildlife and numerous crystal-clear lakes typical of the hills of the Canadian Shield. Summer and winter, visitors can participate in outdoor activities or simply enjoy the tranquility of a protected natural environment. As a nature reserve, the Park offers important educational and research opportunities, featuring rich cultural, historical and recreational attractions. It is linked to the urban capital by beautiful parkways and recreational pathways.

The two photographs below reflect the same section of the Gatineau Parkway in fall and winter. When the snow comes the roadway is closed to vehicles and taken over by cross country skiers.

Aerial view of Mackenzie King Estate at the peak of Gatineau Park's fall colour.

The Mackenzie King Estate is a gift of this celebrated former Prime Minister of Canada. When King arrived in Ottawa in 1900 to begin a long career in the public service, he fell in love with the wilderness scenery just north of the capital that would become Gatineau Park. Starting with a small piece of land on Kingsmere Lake where he built a cottage, King continued to enlarge his holdings until he owned 231 hectares, three summer cottages and a year-round residence. In 1928, Mackenzie King was in his third term as prime minister, and more certain of his political career. He moved to Moorside, a large elegant cottage where he received guests such as Winston Churchill and Charles Lindbergh. When he died, King bequeathed his property in the Gatineau Hills to all Canadians.

Wetlands in Gatineau Park in Fall and Winter.

Part of the 'picturesque' landscaping tradition, the abbey ruins were made up of collected objects that King was fascinated with. "They were placed into the landscape to give it a romantic feel," he explained. Collecting ruins may be an eccentric pastime, but it is hardly a novel one. Royalty and nobility of Europe collected ruins and follies to spread about their estates.

ONTARIO

Spring run-off on the Oxtongue River in the Muskoka resort region north of Toronto.

OTTAWA

In 1857, England's Queen Victoria outraged many in Upper and Lower Canada when she shunned political hotbeds like Toronto, Kingston and Montreal and selected remotely located Ottawa to become the capital. The Queen apparently fell in love with some watercolour sketches she'd seen of the region. Today, Ottawa is a cosmopolitan city with a balance between the presence of government, cultural variety and community life. The main industry here is government, and that translates into a very clean city with many of the city's residents involved in the civil service.

You have to wonder sometimes if the selection of Ottawa as the nation's capital had anything to do with the fact that not only does it act as the 'voice' for all of Canada, but also receives the best and worst weather Canada has to offer. Witness the view of Parliament Hill in the dead of a winter snowstorm. The only colder capital on the planet is Moscow. Winters can be harsh and unforgiving. Compare that to the photo taken from the same location, the grounds of the spectacular Canadian Museum of Civilization in Gatineau Quebec, in the pre-dawn glow of what promises to be a lovely summer's day. These are the waters of Entrance Bay, on the Ottawa River, free-flowing and welcoming, not covered with two feet of ice and snow. But that's Canada, that's Ottawa, and that's winter, and if there's one thing Canadians know how to do, it is adjust and adapt to the seasons.

View of Parliement Hill, silhouetted by the pre-dawn glow of a summer sunrise.

Aerial View of Parliament Hill as RCMP hot air balloon floats above the Canada Day crowds celebrating the July 1st holiday that commemorates the founding of Canada in 1867. Entrance locks of the Rideau Canal can be seen in the right foreground.

Band of the Ceremonial Guard passing the War Memorial following a performance of their Changing the Guard on the lawn of Parliament Hill.

The Royal cipher, the initials of E II R - Queen of Canada gleam on the polished mace of the Drum Major of the Ceremonial Guard.

Two stars of Ottawa's annual Canadian Tulip Festival held each May.

92 Ontario

Parliament Hill is the centrepiece of Ottawa. Visitors are free to walk the spacious lawn presided over by the 300-foot-tall Peace Tower. The Centre Block as it stands today was completed in 1927. The original, completed in 1866, was a victim of fire in 1916. The "Hill" has not only been a place of governance, but a public place of celebration, renewal, protest and peace since the beginning of Confederation.

The heart and soul of Ottawa is undoubtedly the Byward Market. Smaller in size now than in its heyday of fresh farm produce being hawked by street vendors, the market has been a meeting, gathering and shopping place ever since there's been an Ottawa. The flavour of the original market is still in evidence today, and you can still get fresh produce. Much of the original market area has been transformed into charming shops, boutiques and restaurants.

If the Byward Market is the heart and soul of the city, the Rideau Canal is its main artery. Rife with boaters and shore walkers in the summer, the canal is the mainstay of Ottawa's annual Winterlude. At just over 10 kilometres, it's billed as the world's longest skating rink. Locals can't wait until the canal is frozen. Many skate to work and school on it, and you haven't been to Ottawa unless you've skated the canal in winter and sampled a delicious "Beaver Tail"!

Peace Tower on Parliament Hill during the Canadian Tulip Festival.

Main market building at the centre of the Byward Market.

Tour boat begins cruise on the Rideau Canal with the Chateau Laurier and Westin hotels and the Congress Centre anchoring the background.

In winter, Ottawa transforms its famous canal into the world's longest skating rink. This is the same section pictured at left.

TORONTO

Canada's largest city and multicultural melting pot stands proudly on the Lake Ontario shoreline. It seems Toronto is forever re-inventing and redesigning itself to keep pace with the times. Toronto is a financial, industrial, commercial, technological and entertainment focal point for Canada. A modern city, Toronto still has landmarks from its past and strives to preserve that history while advancing into the future. Tens of thousands of people live in the downtown core and along the waterfront. Worldwide, Toronto has a reputation as a clean, friendly and very safe cosmopolitan city.

At 1,815 feet, or 553.33 metres, the CN Tower, a communications facility, is considered to be the world's tallest free-standing structure. Completed in 1989, Skydome was the world's first stadium with a fully retractable roof, and is home to Major League Baseball's Toronto Blue Jays and the Canadian Football League's Toronto Argonauts.

For much of the 20th century, the famous Royal York Hotel stood guard on the waterfront as the tallest building in the British Commonwealth. Today, after a building boom that began in the 1970s, you can barely make out this historic landmark. If you look very closely (inset photo top right), it's the building with the small green dome, just to the left of those black bank towers.

Twilight view of Toronto skyline from Centre island.

Aerial view of Harbourfront.

Ontario

Three boys up early to experience the magic of a Lake Ontario sunrise.

Woman sharing beautiful summer morning on Kew Beach with her dog.

Members of "The Audience", Michael Snow's wonderful sculpture at the entrance to SkyDome, seem to be pointing out the CN Tower to passers by.

Toronto is a city of great neighbourhoods, tree-lined parks, 14 beaches, a wonderfully developed waterfront including a biking and hiking trail extending from Oakville in the West to Whitby in the east. Despite the hustle and bustle of a city of 2.5 million people with another 2 million in the metro area, it's still easy to find a quiet spot on the beach, or a place to watch the beauty of a sunset, all within the city limits.

Most people who haven't been to Toronto relate the city to one BIG thing; the CN Tower. Completed in 1977, it has a very popular public observatory at the 1.465 foot level, which includes a glass floor. Only the brave step onto it to peer straight down − some 447 metres. The more timid revel in the view of Niagara Falls. On a clear day, the mist from the cascades can be seen some 75 kilometres away.

The Skydome had its heyday in the early 1990's when baseball's Blue Jays won back-to-back World Series' Championships. Skydome is also home to a hotel, located directly over—and looking out to—centre field. It celebrated its opening with a gala in June of 1989. With the roof wide open and hundreds of performers on stage, the skies opened, and the rain poured in!

Toronto Blue Jays in action on a beautiful summer afternoon at SkyDome.

Toronto islands ferry about to depart the city for one of the terminals of the Toronto Islands.

Water plays a big part in the life of the city. The Toronto islands are a key part of summer in the city, with a respite to tranquility just a 15-minute ferry ride from downtown. The islands feature the Centreville amusement park, hiking and biking trails, quiet picnic areas, and a residential area where over 100 homeowners live year-round. Oh, one other thing, Hanlon's Point has become famous for Toronto's first nude beach…if you dare!

Old warehouses and factories have been converted to the Harbourfront Centre, another focal point for shops, restaurants, bars and cafés. Harbourfront comes alive in the summer with street performers, festivals, celebrations and special events. it's also a great place to just stroll along the waterfront—vibrant city on one side, Lake Ontario on the other.

Historic steam powered ferry "Trillium" shares narrow passage from Lake Ontario into Toronto's inner harbour with sailboat.

Young girl enjoying her ice cream cone as she follows the progress of a radio-controlled model of a Canadian Navy frigate.

The Amsterdam Bridge named in honour of one of Toronto's twin cities, connects Harbourfront Centre with the old Pier 4, now known as John Quay.

Autumn leaves at the peak of their Fall brilliance in High Park.

The city boasts one of the world's best transit systems, including a subway second to none. Visitors are often amazed when they first see Toronto's streetcars. Powered by electricity and run on rails in the streets, these pollution-free vehicles are an important cog in Toronto's mass transit grid, complementing the subway, bus and light rail systems. And Toronto's streetcars are a tourist attraction in themselves, in that the city is the only place in Canada where they are still in daily use.

Streetcars making their way west on King Street.

Located close to downtown, High Park is one of those getaway places in the middle of the city. Nature provides a different signature each season, and certainly a walk on a crisp colourful autumn day can match lying under the canopy of shade provided by these same trees on a hot Toronto summer afternoon.

Galleria of BCE Place. The old Commercial Bank of the Midland District was moved from another location and artfully incorporated into the design of this complex.

Queen's Park, home to the Ontario Legislature.

Millions of visitors each year are drawn to the city. The theatre district is on par with the best in the world and the stage's top artists perform here regularly. The nightlife is alive with something for everyone and neighbourhoods like Chinatown, Little Italy, Greek Town, and the city's annual Caribbean Festival celebrate the city's diverse population. it's a city where the old is preserved while the new is embraced.

Located in downtown Toronto, Queen's Park has been home to the provincial legislature for over a century. Completed in 1892, the sandstone structure stands at the head of University Avenue, one of the widest downtown streets of any city in North America. If you're thinking of visiting Queen's Park, or going for a walk up University Avenue, taking in the vast expanse of the city, this is the way to go.

More than 400,000 visitors a year visit Casa Loma.

The Gooderham Building, known locally as the "Flatiron Building" because of its unique shape, anchors the west flank of the busy St. Lawrence Market area.

ONTARIO WINE COUNTRY

The morning mist breaks and you find yourself strolling through the vast, lush, green vineyards of…..Ontario? You bet! Much has changed since the first Ontario winery opened on Lake Erie's Pelee Island, the most southern point in Canada, in 1866. Located in roughly the same latitude as the Bordeaux Region of southern France and wine regions of Italy, Spain and California, the province today boasts of three main wine producing areas where climate is key. Pelee Island, the north shore of Lake Erie and perhaps the most famous Ontario wine region surrounding Niagara-on-the-Lake, produce 90% of all the grapes used in Canadian wine production. Wines produced are world class and consistent medal winners in international wine competitions. Wine tours have become major tourist draws where visitors can learn first-hand how Ontario wines have earned their world class reputation. And Canadian winters contribute to our growing reputation as one of the world's best ice wine producers with frozen grapes and their precious juices picked from the vine in the dead of a winter night.

Niagara Falls

In 1678, French Father Louis Hennepin was looking for a route to the Mississippi River. Along the way, he became the first European to see what is one of the greatest natural wonders in the world. Niagara Falls was first settled by the Seneca Indians hundreds of years before Father Hennepin would arrive.

The Falls were formed over 13 thousand years ago when glaciers retreated from this part of Ontario. In their lifetime, the Falls have retreated just over 11 kilometres and one day in the far-off future, this site will be little more than a river's rapids. But today, 150 million litres of Niagara River water thunder over the falls every minute on their journey downstream to Lake Ontario.

Maid Of The Mist approaches Horseshoe Falls.

Boat tours to the base of the Falls on a vessel aptly named *Maid of the Mist* began in 1846. If you're looking to get very wet, but up close and personal with the Falls, this is the way to do it. To be sure, Niagara Falls has its carnival side, but the Falls and areas along the Niagara River are well preserved natural attractions that overpower what man has created. Over 12 million tourists visit the Falls on the Canadian side every year, and before the digital revolution, more film was sold at Niagara Falls than anywhere else in the world!

The Falls consist of two main drops, the American Falls entirely on the U.S. side of the border and the more spectacular Horseshoe Falls on the Canadian side. The Horseshoe Falls have a drop of 177 feet off a curved crest of 2,215 feet. In 1901, 63-year old school teacher Anna Taylor became the first person to go over the falls in a barrel and survive. Not all who have tried this curious feat over the years have been so lucky and today

Somehow, during the settlement and development of Niagara Falls, it became known as the "honeymoon capital of the world" and, to this day, tens of thousands of newlyweds still flock to the Falls to celebrate their nuptials.

View of the Canadian (left) and American Falls (right) from the observation decks perched on the very brink of each of the catapults.

View of the American and Canadian Falls from the Skylon Tower

VOYAGEURS

Voyageurs or "coureurs de bois" navigating rapids on the Ottawa River. Francis Hopkins / National Archives of Canada / C-002774

No one was more responsible for exploring the new country of Canada than those called the *Voyageurs*. These woodsmen paddled and guided many explorers and fur traders through unknown waterways in the frontier west of Montreal. They travelled in large birchbark canoes using native interpreters. Their expeditions could last several weeks, several months or several years. These voyageurs were drawn from the parishes and seigneuries along the St. Lawrence River and were selected mainly for their physical stature. They had to be short – under five and a half feet – to fit into their allotted space in the canoe. They also had to be physically capable of enduring endless 12-hour days of hard physical labour and the harsh weather of the Canadian shield country that would be their home.

Many of these men, signing up to escape the boredom of rural life, had no idea what they were getting into. But they were a tough, courageous bunch, although not particularly amenable to taking orders. Voyageurs did things their way, and their way was obviously the right way. Explorers like Pierre de Le Verendrye, Alexander MacKenzie, David Thompson and Simon Fraser all used the voyageurs, while trading companies like the North West Company and the Hudson's Bay Company relied on them in their business of gathering furs. In search of new places to trap and trade, their canoes ventured ever westward. Their routes included the Ottawa, Mattawa and French Rivers and into Lake Huron.

Georgian Bay shoreline near Parry Sound. J. David Andrews

Aerial view of the Canadian Shield granite of Georgian Bay.

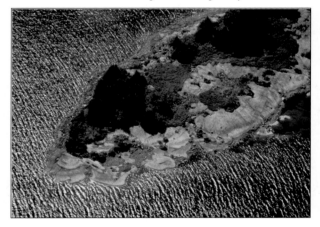

Paddler enjoying a magic moment on Pine Lake in Muskoka, while concentrating on catching a trout for breakfast.

Beyond Lake Superior, past the end of the Great Lakes, they explored as far west as the foothills of the Rocky Mountains and south as far as the Mississippi River. In the process they were the first to map out much of the continent. Today, many of the rivers first navigated by voyageurs remain just as calm or unruly as when they were first paddled. Canoeists and kayakers can follow in the wake of the voyageurs along many of these same routes taken hundreds of years ago. Whitewater rafters seen here along the Ottawa River experience the same ride through wild river rapids as the voyageurs, but with the comfort of knowing a spill into the river won't mean losing all their equipment, food, and quite possibly, their only means of transportation home.

Whitewater rafters and canoeists are both drawn to the rapids of the Ottawa River north of the capital city of Ottawa.

Paddlers enjoying the quiet of early morning on the Madawaska River.

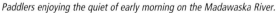

THE NORTH

There's only one thing wrong with this stunning photograph of the Lowell Glacier in Kluane National Park in the southwest corner of the Yukon. The hiker in the picture is not you! The sheer immensity of the Canadian north jumps off the page here. Kluane is also home to Canada's highest peak, Mount Logan, and some of the most extensive icefields outside the polar region. The park is part of a two country, one state, one province, one territory UNESCO World Heritage Site. It joins St. Elias and Glacier Bay National Park in Alaska, and the Taatshenshini-Alsek Wilderness Park in British Columiba as one of the great protected areas in the world. Landscape in the area includes what you see as well as mountain lakes, alpine meadows, tundra and cold swift-flowing rivers and forests of spruce and aspen. The north is a land where man is the intruder. That's something the locals know and visitors must keep in mind. Perhaps Canadian author Farley Mowat knew something when he wrote "There is no authentic report of wolves ever having killed a human being in the Canadian North; although there must have been times when the temptation was well nigh irresistible." After my first visit to the north I was struck by three things: the beauty, the isolation and the beauty of that isolation.

Wolf in the Yukon's Kluane National Park.
T. Hall/Parks Canada/W.11.110.10.01.04

Musk Oxen in Aulavik National Park, Inuvik Region, Northwest Territories.
Wayne Lynch/Parks Canada/12.123.10.01.28

Arctic lichen in Aulavik National Park, Inuvik Region, Northwest Territories.
Wayne Lynch/Parks Canada/12.123.03.05.28

Kettle Lake and McDonald River Valley, Quitinirpaaq National Park on Ellesmere Island in the Qikiqtaaluk Region of Nunavut
Ian MacNeil/Parks Canada/13.02.03.08.67

Hiker expressing awe at his view of the Lowell Glacier in Kluane National Park, Yukon.
Wayne Lynch/Parks Canada 11.110.09.07.26

Dramatic outlook offers heart-stopping view of Virginia Falls in Nahanni (River) National Park, Northwest Territories.
Mike Beedell/Parks Canada/12.120.03.02.29

The images on these pages reflect experienced hikers enjoying four of Canada's more remote National Parks. Back-country trips to these places require more planning and experience than their southern counterparts, but they offer wondrous vistas to those willing to make the extra effort these locales demand.

Summit Lake Area Auyuittuq National Park, Nunavut.
Mike Beedel/Parks Canada/13.03.07.12.02

Climbers on King Trench, Mount Logan expedition, Kluane National Park, Yukon.
Mike Beedel/Parks Canada/11.110.07.08.141

Caribou sharing campsite in Vuntut National Park, Yukon.
Wayne Lynch/Parks Canada/11.112.10.01.69

Quttinirpaaq National Park, Yukon. J. David Andrews/P.C. 13.02.07.04.18

Discovery Harbour from Fort Conger, Quttinirpaaq National Park, Nunavut. Wayne Lynch/Parks Canada/13.02.03.19.68

One can only wonder about the thoughts of the crew of *HMS Discovery* as they wintered here, at the lonely outpost of Fort Conger on the northeastern coast of Ellesmere Island in the winter of 1875-76. As part of the British Arctic Expedition, they explored the north coast of Ellesmere Island and Greenland using man-hauled sledges. Two decades later, Robert Peary refitted the encampment and used it sporadically on his various attempts to reach the North Pole between 1898 and 1909.

These early explorers came sailing thought ice-laden waters aboard wooden ships, overcoming their fear of the crushing ice and the endless darkness of the frigid arctic winters, only to meet the loneliness of months of isolation far from home. Today, modern means of transportation have made Quttinirpaaq National Park in Nunavut easier to access and leave, but it's still a place of discovery, adventure, mystery and isolation.

Paddlers on the Thomsen River, Aulavik, Northwest Territories. Wayne Lynch/Parks Canada/12.123.07.19.19

What kind of people could have lived in a climate like this? it's believed the first Eskimos, a Cree term meaning "eater of raw meat", probably crossed the Bering Strait from Siberia over 4000 years ago. Today, only native people of Arctic Alaska call themselves Eskimo. Native Canadians from the north call themselves *Inuit*, meaning "the people". Living in such a climate requires one to be ingenious, hearty, skillful, thrifty, and—most of all—possessed by a love and respect for the land. Generations have lived here, enduring the cold and the darkness, led by an unwavering faith in their Spirits and Gods. Their survival over thousands of years is a testament to how very well they adapted to the environment.

Lunar eclipse, Kluane National Park. Janet Foster / Masterfile

Today, most Inuit live in villages or settlements. But for years the traditional igloo was home. When you think about it, the concept is brilliant. You could make one anywhere, anytime and the elements were always working for you, not against you. Once the snow blocks are cut and the igloo is built, a lamp is lit inside. The heated air, having no place to escape, begins to slowly melt the interior face of the blocks. The melting effect is quickly concealed again, however, by cold air coming in through the entrance. Thus, each snow block is firmly cemented into place, and once the family moves in, it is only a matter of days until the structure is no longer a snow house, but an icehouse. The igloo has remarkable stability. So strong in fact, that a man could stand on the very top without risk of collapse. And cozy? You bet! No matter what the temperature outside, inside is always just 1 or 2 degrees below freezing.

Polar bear hunting for seals on the Arctic ice cap.
Daryl Benson / Masterfile

Traditional igloo shelter made of blocks of compacted snow, Nunavut. Mike Macri / Masterfile

Winter is also the time the polar Bear is on the prowl. Between freeze-up and break-up, polar bears actively hunt seals on the polar ice pack. When the ice is gone, the bears come ashore and some move several kilometres inland. Exceedingly fat from their winter of eating, polar bears spend most of the summer sleeping to conserve energy.

Polar bears are one of the wonders of the north, and have a loveable and cuddly look to them. But beware. Never approach a Polar bear. In fact, head in the other direction quickly if you see one in the wild. They are very dangerous, meat-eating creatures. Truly a case of looks being deceiving!

Northern Lights, Nunavut. Wayne Lynch / Masterfile

Only five per cent of the world's population has seen the northern lights. And to see them is truly a sight to behold. You can observe the *aurora borealis* in the northern night sky in Canada's western provinces and into Ontario's north if conditions are right. To be sure, to see the aurora anywhere is spectacular, to see it in Canada's north, takes your breath away.

The northern lights are created when the billions and billions of electrically charged ions emitted from the sun every day are pushed toward earth by solar winds and pulled here by gravity. When these ions collide with the earth, they are directed to the north and south poles. The colour of the aurora is created when the ions mix with gas atoms to give off light.

Northern lights, Churchill, Manitoba. Mike Macri / Masterfile

Different gases mean different colours of light. I saw the northern lights in a setting about 50 kilometres outside Yellowknife in the Northwest Territories. On a cold February night, I watched the aurora, not in a far away sky, but dancing right above my head – spinning, swirling, lingering for a while, then changing shape and moving away.

When you see them in the north you feel you can reach out and touch them, almost *hear* them. You can watch them approach, see the show, catch your breath, and wait for the next show to begin. On a good night, that next show is just a few seconds away.

You notice the caption says *abandoned* grain elevator. Once a staple of the prairie landscape, the traditional grain elevators pictured here have given way to new steel versions. Grain elevators are used to weigh, clean and store grain and this classic wooden structure was as much a part of the prairies as the grain itself. But not anymore.

Abandoned grain elevator, Alberta.

PRAIRIES

In the 1930's, almost 6000 grain elevators graced the land throughout Alberta, Saskatchewan and Manitoba. Today, less than 850 remain and they are an endangered species. In the agricultural economy of the west, villages grew up around the elevator. With industrialization and the move to the cities, many of these villages – and their elevators – disappeared. For the grain business to continue to flourish, the modern, economical and practical course was the one to take.

Prairie wheat field, Saskatchewan.

Still, when you think of Canadiana, and symbols of Canada, the prairie grain elevator is a living memorial to a bygone era so critical to the growth of this country.

The prairies are as much a part of the diverse Canadian mosaic as the mountains of Alberta and British Columbia, the great lakes of Ontario and the rocky shoreline of Newfoundland and Labrador. In the 19th century, Europeans and Americans began migrating to urban centres. No longer growing their own wheat, these families needed a new source for their bread staple, and the new country of Canada was poised to become the "breadbasket of the world".

While prairie agriculture is characterized by rolling fields of wheat, is the regions beef industry is equally important..

Wheat changed Canada. Tens of thousands of Europeans migrated to the prairies, lured by the Canadian government's offer of free land in the west and a new start. These settlers quickly realized that wheat was the one crop the land would support and wheat was what the world wanted. By 1930, Canada and Canadian wheat were a major player in feeding the world. It takes a special kind of farmer to work the wheat fields of the prairies.

Canada is full of them. Through isolation, drought, frightful winters and sweltering summers, these men and women have always displayed an unwavering resolve to carve out a living from the land. Their reward is the satisfaction to be found in overcoming any obstacle to bring that crop to market. For most their farms have been in the family for generations, and it's the only life they know, the only life they want.

Signature wheat fields that characterize Canada's prairie landscape.

Kim Anton and cow boss, Bud Maynard working cattle
on the OH Ranch, Longview, Alberta.

Les Ivan checking mother cows and calves in the hill country of the Quilchena Cattle Company near Merritt, British Columbia.

THE COWBOY

Ranching is a form of agriculture that is relatively young, having its roots in the American State of Texas. After that country's Civil War ended in 1865, thousands of soldiers from both sides drifted west to seek their fortunes. Already skilled horsemen, these veterans quickly adopted the ways of the Mexican *vaqueros* and learned they could round up stray cattle to earn a few dollars. After the vast buffalo herds were all but wiped out these cowboys as they came to be called, began rounding up large herds of Texas cattle, driving them north to the rich grasslands of Wyoming, Montana and the Canadian territory that would become the province of Alberta. Here they were fattened and shipped to the vast beef markets of the east. A few mother cows were kept back to be bred in the spring and the seeds of the modern ranch were sewn.

Hollywood films elevated the lowly cowboy to near legendary status and people from all over the world continue to be drawn to the North American west where they are surprised to discover that real cowboys still work cattle on horseback, employing the rope and branding iron of the old west.

Sure you will see fancy, four-wheel drive pickups and even the odd helicopter involved in the cattle business today. But, as one rancher put it; "A good horse costs about the same as a tractor transmission, they always start in the morning and they never get stuck". "If it ain't broke, why fix it?", seems to apply here. In our modern, fast-paced world it is somehow comforting to come across a way of life rich in tradition and old fashioned values. Today's rancher, like his predecessors, still battles market cycles in beef prices, the banker, disease and drought and he still looks to the sky for any sign of the rain he needs to mix with sunshine and grass so he can turn it into beef. And he would never consider any other way of earning a living.

Grant Armstrong and Dewey Hale heading home.
Bow Valley Cattle Company, Bassano, Alberta.

WINNIPEG

Winds pick up speed as they barrel across the flat prairie and when they hit the buildings and skyscrapers in the downtown Winnipeg business core, they orchestrate a dance, which can create both hazardous and wondrous situations.   Aerial view of Winnipeg's Portage & Main.

Founded in the late 1730's as the Red River Colony, Winnipeg quickly emerged as a hub of the burgeoning fur trade, largely because of its location. Strategically situated at the junction of the Red and Assiniboine rivers, arterial highways for the early explorers, the colony was a natural location for a fur trading post. Location again helped the settlement when the railway and early road system were drawn to Winnipeg because of its position south of the rugged terrain of the Canadian Shield. Today, Winnipeg, the "Gateway to the West", is a vibrant city with a population approaching 800,000.

The Red and Assiniboine Rivers converge at "The Forks", an area that was central to the fur trade. But with the advent of the industrial revolution and the coming of the railway early in the 20th century, the homes and businesses on the north bank of the Assiniboine River gave way to massive rail yards and associated industrial activity.

Today The Forks is once again the city's favourite gathering place. Rebirth of the area came in the form of shops, walks and historic buildings reclaimed when the city's rail activity was relocated east of the downtown core. And it was at this location that an archeological dig uncovered artifacts indicating that The Forks was a seasonal meeting place for Aboriginal people over 6,000 years ago!

The city features what arguably must be the most famous intersection in all of Canada: Portage and Main. Famous – not for an historical event or sensational happening – but rather for having the reputation of being the windiest, and in the dead of a prairie winter, coldest location in the country.

Winnipeg is the capital of Manitoba, and the legislative building is situated on 12 hectares of garden and parkscape. Be sure to look to the top of the legislative dome. There stands the famous "Golden Boy", refurbished, and rededicated by the Queen in 2002.

Ruins of the St. Boniface Cathedral.

Winnipeg's famous "Golden Boy".

Golden Boy has quite a history. Sculpted by Charles Gardet of Paris, the ship carrying the statue from France was diverted during the First World War to become a troop carrier.

Finally, after two years and many Atlantic crossings, the statue was placed where it stands today, a torch in one hand, a sheaf of wheat in the other..

Province of Manitoba Legislature.

The Red and Assiniboine Rivers converge at "The Forks", an area that was central to the fur trade.

"Free land! And plenty of it!" That was the clarion cry of the federal government at the end of the 19th century. With the completion of the railway in 1885, Canada was joined from sea to sea. But the prairies remained a vast expanse of millions and millions of acres of grassy tableland just waiting to be settled and put to the plough. Starting in the 1870's, the government of the day worked vigorously to promote mass immigration by appealing to the landless masses in eastern Canada and Europe.

Steamship lines were given bonuses of five dollars for each head of a family they delivered to Canadian shores and two dollars for everyone else. The lure of free land proved to be irresistible. Who could pass up an offer like "125,000 FREE farms of 160 acres each, located along Canadian Northern Railway lines"? This massive effort worked like a charm. Thousands from Eastern Canada, Britain and Europe made the trek west.

Ruins of old house and barn reflect the hardships faced by the early settlers who migrated from Europe with dreams of a new life in Canada.

The rules were simple. To own land under the "Dominion Lands Act" the settler had to break 30 of 160 acres, and farm 20 acres within three years. Second, he had to build a home on the land and third, the settler had to live on the land for at least 6 months of the year. Once these conditions were met a $10 filing fee was paid and the settler received his prized deed. But life was not easy on the prairies. It was a land that had never been farmed and families were totally isolated with no support communities in the beginning. Newcomers had to learn to live off the land and many times that situation proved to be one of life or death. Winters were particularly cold and harsh while summers were often sweltering and dry. The infamous "dust bowl" of the early 1930's ended many a dream. Through all the hardships though, most persevered and, to this day, there are many third and fourth generation farmers on the same ground their forefathers broke over 100 years ago.

SASKATOON

South Saskatchewan River and downtown area of Saskatoon.

The landmark Delta Bessborough Hotel.

The largest city in Saskatchewan, with a population just under 200,000, Saskatoon is known as the "city of bridges". The South Saskatchewan River meanders through the city and a total of seven spans keep things connected. John Lake founded the city in 1882 as a temperance colony and named it Saskatoon, after tasting a handful of purple berries that grew in abundance along the river that the Cree called *misaskquatoomina*. To this day, the Saskatoon berry is a fruit staple all over the province. Saskatoon is also the point the province begins to change. Prairie land extends north to the city, but it's also the gateway to tens of thousands of lakes and pristine forest in northern Saskatchewan. Little known fact: 50% of the province is covered by trees, and there are upwards of 100 thousand fresh water lakes!

Aerial view of wheat field in southern Saskatchewan.

REGINA

Downtown Regina and Victoria Park as seen from the roof of the Hotel Saskatchewan Radisson Plaza.

Founded in 1882 when the railway came through, the capital of Saskatchewan was first named Pile Of Bones. Thank goodness a few years later, Princess Louise, the wife of Canada's Governor General, renamed the city Regina, in honour of her mother, Queen Victoria. Regina sits in the heart of the prairies, its two unique glass skyscrapers dominating the downtown core. it's a city literally surrounded by agriculture and embodies the spirit of the prairies. Regina is also home to one of the largest urban parks in North America, the Wascana Centre. At 930 hectares, the park surrounds Wascana Lake and is home to the provincial legislative buildings, University of Saskatchewan, Saskatchewan Science Centre and the Diefenbaker Homestead, the boyhood home of former Canadian Prime Minister John Diefenbaker, (1957-1963).

Saskatchewan Legislative Assembly Building.

West-bound, container freight passing wheat cars on siding near Regina at sunrise.

What's this? A desert tucked away in the southwest corner of Saskatchewan? Well, it may not be exactly a desert, but it certainly is an area of the province with arid conditions, displaying many of the characteristics of desert terrain. Located near Sceptre, Saskatchewan, the Great Sand Hills almost seem out of place in a country like Canada. Reaching 10 to 12 metres in height, these magnificent dunes stand out like islands in the vast desert-like scrub terrain.

Only 1% of this 1900 square kilometre area contains sand dunes, and at times you can be standing on one and not see another. But sand is not the only attraction in the area. Separating the dunes is ground that is a little hilly and covered in vegetation more typical of the American southwest. A wide assortment of hardy plants shares the space here and includes many varieties of shrubs, prairie grasses and cacti. Mule deer and antelope can often be seen at the edge of the grassland along the sand hills.

Dunes of The Great Sand Hills of Saskatchewan. Daryl Benson / Masterfile

Like the sands of the great deserts of the world, this landscape is constantly changing with each gust of wind, drop of rain or winter snowfall. In fact, studies show these dunes can travel about 3 to 4 metres per year, leaving what are known as dune tracks. There are upwards of 20 different sand dune formations here, and the area is also an archaeological gold mine. Over 11,000 years ago, Indian hunters trapped buffalo in the area, using the sand as a device to slow the animals down. The Great Sand Hills also hold a treasure below the surface: natural gas.

This is not the only area of great sand dunes in Saskatchewan. At the northern extreme of the province, where Lake Athabasca separates Saskatchewan from the Northwest Territories, lies the Athabasca Sand Dunes Provincial Park. This remote, hard-to-reach area is home to the world's most northerly major sand dunes. Some in this park rise to 30 metres and you can also find 10 species of plants found nowhere else in the world. Many Canadians envision Saskatchewan as a flat, wheat-growing province from top to bottom. Nothing could be further from the truth!

If you're not used to seeing them, coming upon a herd will take you by surprise. The first thing is the double take, and then you realize that yes – bison, often colloquially called "buffalo". Actually you're lucky to see them. Once millions and millions roamed the plains but the killing of the 1800s reduced the numbers of these magnificent animals to less than 1000 by 1879. Extinction was a definite possibility.

But the buffalo survived and upwards of 150 thousand find a home in Canada, where there are over 1400 bison producers today. Plains Indians hunted the buffalo, and relied on them not just for meat, but for shelter, clothing and a source of utensils and tools. Nothing was wasted after a kill, even the "cow chips" were used for fueling fires.

A mature bison bull can weight up to 2000 pounds, while a mature bison cow would check in at about 1100 lbs. Perhaps the most surprising thing about a buffalo is its speed. They can run up to 50 kilometres per hour! This speed made their capture a difficult chore for the Plains Indians, who would counter it by cornering the buffalo and driving them off tall cliffs to their death.

Sundanace buffalo Ranch, Irvine, Alberta.

A visit to Head–Smashed–In Buffalo Jump Interpretive Centre, south of Calgary, will give you the whole story.

I've been lucky enough to criss-cross Canada many times. Because of that I'm often asked the almost unanswerable question...what *one* place would you recommend visiting? Canada has so much to offer. Mountains, glaciers, rivers, lakes, forest, sea coast, prairie, pristine wilderness and rugged, rocky terrain. I've been lucky enough to see all that. But if I had to recommend just one place, it would be here: Dinosaur Provincial Park just outside Brooks, Alberta. You'll understand why, once you see it.

Unique "hoodoo" formations characteristic of the badlands of the Red Deer River valley east of Drumheller. A hoodoo is a pillar of sediment carved by wind and water erosion. Because the underlying rock is more susceptible to the forces of nature, it erodes more quickly than the much harder surface rock (also known as the cap stone).

About two hours east of Calgary, Alberta, the gently rolling prairie grasslands suddenly drop off, plunging the visitor into a whole other world of hoodoos, pinnacles, coulees and buttes. Many who visit these badlands for the first time describe this sudden transition as if they have taken a wrong turn and somehow ended up on the moon. Strange land formations rise up on all sides, sculpted by wind and water into hauntingly beautiful shapes sunbathed in terra cotta, bronze and amber.

A trip to Dinosaur Provincial Park is also a 75 million-year foray back in time. This region was then a subtropical paradise populated by turtles, crocodiles and sharks - and featuring lush vegetation similar to the coastal plains of the southeastern United States today.

Here, on the shores of the Bearpaw Sea, dinosaurs once hunted and mated and ultimately met their demise, leaving an amazingly rich fossil and bone record for us to discover today. So far, there have been 35 kinds of dinosaur species unearthed in the park, and it's anyone's guess how many more are out there. You can visit a display of excavated bones, covered and preserved exactly where they were found. And throughout the park, you'll also find stakes with numbers on them, each representing a dinosaur find.

In 1979, Dinosaur Provincial Park was designated a UNESCO World Heritage Site. World Heritage sites are established for the lasting protection of irreplaceable cultural and natural heritage resources of international significance.

Dinosaur Provincial Park near Drumheller.

CALGARY

Calgary skyline bathed in the first light of a summer sunrise.

If there's a city in Canada that embodies the "spirit of the west", it's Calgary. The most famous of rodeos, the Calgary Stampede, is held every year in July and, for 10 days, everybody's a cowboy or cowgirl. (That's a requirement by the way pardner, and there's no getting around it!) Billed as the largest outdoor show on earth, the event celebrates the *cowboy way* with its centrepiece rodeo featuring bronc and bull riding, barrel racing, roping, and the ever-popular chuckwagon races. The Stampede has long been a tourist attraction and it, along with a thriving ranching industry and the discovery of oil nearby, put Calgary on the map for the rest of Canada. Nestled into the foothills of the Rocky Mountains on its western boundary, the city sits literally at the end of the prairies. Visitors driving into Calgary from the east always marvel at that first view of the skyline as it suddenly reveals itself over a small rise on the Trans Canada Highway.

The world took notice In 1988 when Calgary staged one of the most successful Winter Olympic Games ever. For the length of those games, a torch burned atop the Calgary Tower and is still illuminated on special occasions. The tower rises 191 metres or 621 feet, giving a panoramic view of the entire city; prairie to the east, ranch land to the south and the spectacular Rocky Mountains to the west. Calgary was founded as a North West Mounted Police outpost in 1875. But things changed forever in 1914 when oil was discovered south of the city, and again in 1947 when the giant Leduc field came in near Edmonton to the north. Those discoveries fueled the growth of Calgary, transforming its agricultural economy almost overnight. Today the city boasts that it is home to the second largest number of corporate head offices in the country and its industrial base, comprised of energy, agriculture, manufacturing, tourism and technology all contribute to its thriving economy. What's the secret to Calgary's success? It has never forgotten its western roots.

Calf ropers in action, Calgary Stampede.

THE CANADIAN ROCKIES

I think it really hits you right here, with this picture, on this page. Beautiful. The Rocky Mountains, in all their majesty, acting as a western bookend to a shelf of scenery no other country in the world can offer. You've journeyed this far though our pages and what have you seen? Just about everything! From oceans to icebergs, from rocks to riches, from lakes and forests, wilderness and tundra, sandscapes and prairies, history and hard times, spirit and co-operation, discovery and disappointment, the Canadian landscape is unlike any other. So much to see, yet so much unseen. And you still have British Columbia and the Pacific Ocean to look forward to.

To top it all off, you've just hit what might be Canada's signature postcard to the world, the mountains. I've always thought you have to see these mountains in as many ways as you can. By air, by car, on foot, by boat, canoe or kayak, bicycle, horseback, ski, and above all, by train. These ranges and peaks never move, yet they are constantly changing. Mountains are seasonal, ever maintaining an imposing presence on the landscape, while at the same time adjusting to wind, rain, snow, sun, and man. Just as these mountains can be the friendliest place on earth, so can they be the harshest.

Sunshine Meadows, Banff National Park. Miles Ertman / Masterfile

With all of Canada's diverse geography, it's amazing how much of what we've seen is contained in this one shot. The fresh water lakes, rocks, the valley, the colour of the trees, the forest, the tree line, snow, flat lands, the river, the meadow, and of course, the mountains as they reach out to touch the sky. Have you ever sat by a mountain stream and watched water running past, so clear that you can make out the outline of every pebble on the bottom? You should. Have you ever hiked to the top of one of the many accessible peaks and spread your arms in disbelief at the vista that is revealed to you? You should. Have you ever stood in a place where all you can see is the land as it was tens of thousands, if not millions, of years ago? You can, and you should!

There's a ski area near Golden B.C. called the Kicking Horse Resort. If you take the gondola there to the top, winter or summer, you will find yourself at an elevation of about 7700 feet. And if you stop for lunch at the Eagle's Eye restaurant you will be dining at the highest eatery in Canada. From this singular vantage point you can see the mountains of Yoho National Park, Banff National Park, Kootenay National Park and Glacier National Park. It's breathtaking and the beauty of it is that there are hundreds of views just like it, some discovered, some still waiting for discovery and some perhaps, never to be discovered.

View of Bow River from the Trans-Canada Highway.

The beauty of both highway routes leaving Banff – heading west to British Columbia on the Trans Canada Highway or north to Jasper on the Icefields Parkway – is how much you can see from the road. And there are plenty of places to stop and just soak it all in. So bring lots of film and take home lots of memories.

Considered one of the most scenic highways in the world, the 230-kilometre -ong Icefields Parkway offers stunning vistas of waterfalls, emerald lakes, alpine meadows, advancing glaciers and snow-capped peaks. The Parkway follows the headwaters of three major rivers and crosses two major passes en route to the town of Jasper.

One of many small lakes along the Icefields Parkway.

SPIRIT ISLAND

Around the world, Spirit Island has come to symbolize the beauty of the Canadian Rockies. This special place can only be reached by water as the lake is rimmed on all sides by rugged, snow-capped peaks. The most popular route is via the motorized tour boats of Maligne Tours, based in nearby Jasper. During the half-hour cruise to Spirit Island the captain and crew will tell you about the geology, history, wildlife and glaciology of this spectacular area.

Spirit Island, Maligne Lake, Jasper National Park.
Daryl Benson / Masterfile

EDMONTON

The development of the City of Edmonton, from Hudson's Bay Company trading post in 1795, to presentday metropolis, is a microcosm of the development of this part of Canada as a whole. Today Edmonton is an industrial city, thanks largely to the discovery of oil just south of town in the late 1940s. In the late 1800s, Edmonton was the last supply point for prospectors heading to the Klondike with golden dreams dancing in their heads. For most, those dreams turned to nightmares, but what was a bust for prospectors, became a boom for Edmonton. Many, who returned from the Klondike empty-handed settled in Edmonton and, in ten short years, the city grew to six times its previous size. Because of this, the city was made the capital of Alberta in 1905. Its strategic location earned it the reputation as the "gateway to the north", a title that it retains to this day.

When you mention Edmonton to most people, they think of the West Edmonton Mall, one of the largest indoor shopping centres in the world. The massive complex contains hundreds of stores, several hotels, a full-size hockey rink, amusement park with a very large 'outdoor-sized' roller coaster, a hard-to-believe-until-you-see-it indoor water park, complete with giant, tropical wave pool and water slides, dolphin shows, a pirate cove, themed streets and restaurants galore. This mall is one of the few places where you are likely to drop, before you've completed the shopping part!

Visitors to this northern Alberta city can't help but be amazed at the amount of green space city fathers and forefathers have preserved for their citizens. The North Saskatchewan River runs through the heart of the city and, at 7,340 hectares or 18,300 acres, Edmonton's river valley parkland is one of the largest areas of urban green space in any North American city.

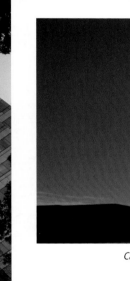

Alberta Legislative building.

Heart of Edmonton's business district.

Tropical wave pool, West Edmonton Mall.

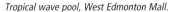

Canadian Petroleum Discovery Centre, Devon, Alberta.

The turning point for the modern city of Edmonton occurred on February 13th, 1947, some 40 kilometres to the south. After drilling 133 dry wells, Imperial Oil struck it rich with well number 134. On that bitter cold day, Vern "Dry Hole" Hunter and his crew changed the fate of Edmonton, and all of Alberta, forever. First spurting water, then drilling mud, and finally oil, Leduc Number One well announced the discovery of the 200 million-barrel Leduc oilfield. In the 25 years following the Leduc oil discovery, the population of Edmonton quadrupled! It was the first in a series of postwar oil and gas finds that forever changed the face of Alberta.

Near the oilfields, existing towns grew with the industry, and entirely new towns were built. Virtually overnight, petroleum and petrochemical refining took over Alberta's economy, bringing thousands of new jobs and job-seekers to the province. And it all started one cold February day in 1947.

Crew on servicing rig #10 (Performance Drilling) experiencing a little "kick".

Things started quite inauspiciously in 1901 with the first oil discovery on Cameron Creek in today's Waterton Lakes National Park. The oil exploration seed had been planted and drilling rigs would became a common sight throughout the province. But it would be more than ten years later that everything changed when Alberta's first producing well, Dingman #1 came in. It was 1914 and overnight, the sleepy little town of Turner Valley south of Calgary, was transformed into a boom town and the economy of Alberta was forever changed. After the Second World War, as the Turner Valley reserves were beginning to dry up, Imperial Oil's Leduc #1 came in and a vast new reserve was discovered just south of Edmonton. Through the last half of the twentieth century something called the oil sands slowly emerged as the new giant in Alberta's oil and gas industry and momentous change was afoot.

John McQuarrie, ***The Alberta Oil Patch*** (Magic Light Publishing 2010)

North America runs on oil, coal, and natural gas. Although a larger share of our needs will be met through increased use of hydro-electricity, wind, solar, nuclear, and other forms of renewables, fossil fuels will continue to play an important role in our nation's energy mix in the foreseeable future. Securing that future means finding a secure supply. And one growing solution is the natural bitumen deposits that make up Canada's oil sands and the recent advances in shale deposits.

In terms of overall oil reserves, Canada's 174 billion barrels is third only to Venezuela and Saudi Arabia. Oil sands account for over 97 per cent of that vast reserve: 169 billion barrels of oil, with the potential for over 100 years of production. The value of Canada's energy exports in 2012 was $104 billion, accounting for 6 per cent of the country's GDP and 26 per cent of all Canadian exports. Statistics Canada

THE OIL PATCH

Pump jack in the foothill country of Turner Valley, Alberta.

Syncrude's Mildred Lake mine in the oil sands near Fort McMurray.

Long term supply is critical in a world where supply risks are growing, whether due to declining production from a once reliable source, an unstable geo-political climate, or uncertainties in key oil producing regions.

Forty years ago, global oil reserves were largely the domain of the investor-owned international oil companies, based principally in the United States and accounting for 85 per cent of the world's reserves. Today, 80 per cent of world oil reserves are owned by national oil companies belonging to foreign governments. Of the remaining 20 per cent, Canada accounts for 55% of the reserves available for development. Politically stable, Canada has a reputation for technical and contractual reliability as well as high environmental standards, and offers abundant supplies of reliable, affordable energy and the requisite delivery and distribution infrastructure.

A note on Green House Gas (GHG) emissions: Total oil sands GHG emissions in 2011 were 55 megatonnes Source: Environment Canada 2013. This is equivalent to 4.3% of the emissions from the U.S. coal-fired power-generation sector in 2011. Oil sands account for 7.8% of Canada's GHG emissions and just over 0.16% (1/630th) of global GHG emissions. Source: Environment Canada 2012 and United Nations Statistical Division.   Canadian Association of Petroleum Producers

In the past, Alberta's economy has been plagued by booms and busts due to the volatile nature of the oil industry. Now that petroleum from the bituminous sands can be processed in an economically sustainable manner, the provincial economy has been able to step off this rollercoaster and onto a stable foundation for the first time in its history.

Skiers are always on the lookout for that perfect powder run. Freshly fallen snow, a crisp, clear sunny day, and the chance to put first tracks in the virgin snow. Dreams like this come true in the mountains of Alberta and British Columbia...daily! The mountains are a winter wonderland for skiers, hikers and adventurers. Heli-skiing whisks skiers to otherwise unreachable areas for that once in a lifetime run. Only those who have made fresh tracks on a mountain fully comprehend what a religious experience it can be. Helicopters also ferry cross-county skiers, mountaineers and hikers to remote, pristine areas for a once in a lifetime experience. Some of the world's greatest ski areas are located here and its not uncommon for resorts to have a base of a couple of hundred centimetres of snow. Many times one has to literally travel through the clouds to get from the base of a resort to the top of the mountain. Getting there is half the fun! Whistler-Blackcomb, one of the top resorts in the world located two hours north of Vancouver, offers the chance to ski on the Blackcomb Glacier. And there's just something about saying you've skied on a glacier that adds to the overall experience.

Blackcomb Mountain, Whistler Ski Resort.
Randy Lincks / Masterfile

Banff Springs Hotel. Miles Ertman / Masterfile

Lake Louise. Alec Pytlowany / Masterfile

Valelmont heli-skiing. Alec Pytlowany / Masterfile

Rain Forest on West Coast Trail near
Pachena Point, Vancouver Island, B.C.
Parks Canada 10.104.03.06.114

BRITISH COLUMBIA

P&O liner passing under Lions Gate Bridge after a week long Alaska cruise.

Sunrise view of Coal Harbour and downtown Vancouver from Stanley Park.

VANCOUVER

Vancouver is a city like no other in Canada. Built where the Coast Range Mountains fall into the sea, it's been a major port for over 100 years. Because of its location, it quickly established itself as a transPacific shipping hub, and as a result, Vancouver's population was already at 100,000 by the year 1900. Today, Vancouver is the major shipping, financial, industrial and cultural centre on Canada's West Coast. The first thing you notice is the geography, followed closely by the sheer physical beauty of the place. Its climate is a major draw, and to some a major drawback! While the presence of the Pacific Ocean generates warm summers and mild, generally snow-free winters, it also produces a little more rain than the rest of Canada experiences.

The rejuvenated Gastown district, one of the oldest in the city, is a major draw with its historic buildings housing a host of shops, restaurants and clubs. The Lions Gate Bridge is one of the most famous in Canada, with its three lanes of traffic. Rush hour determines which direction gets the extra lane. Vancouver hosted Expo 86. The event drew 20 million visitors to the city, making it the most successful world's fair ever.

Stanley Park's Brockton Point bathed in soft light of a Spring sunrise.

Panoramic view of Vancouver over False Creek.

Sunrise on the Burrard Inlet side of Stanley Park – unimproveable!

Prospect Point Lighthouse from the Lions Gate Bridge

Coal Harbour from the Seawall

SEAWALL

If there is ever to be a book or film depicting the world's greatest walks, the nine-kilometre Seawall encircling Stanley Park would be the cover feature or lead by which all others would be judged. We throw out superlatives like magnificent, spectacular and beautiful much too freely in our daily conversations so, when we really need one, they have all been diluted by overuse. A complete circuit here yields vistas of the downtown core, Burrard Inlet, Coal Harbour, the North Shore, Georgia Strait, English Bay, Kitsilano and all the delights of Stanley Park. To spend a sunny day exploring this glorious promenade on foot or by bike is—by itself—worth a flight from anywhere in Canada.

A mother and daughter explore the wonders of the tidal flat exposed at low tide.

PACIFIC RIM

The Pacific Rim is the only National Park Reserve on Vancouver Island. Hugging the Pacific Ocean, the park is divided into three distinct geographical units: Long Beach, the legendary West Coast Trail, and the Broken Group Islands.

Long Beach is a 16-kilometre stretch of sandy beach on the Pacific. The constant roar of the surf sometimes is the only thing soaring eagles hear during flight. But the beach is also a popular tourist destination and a hot spot for surfers. Time the tide right, and your pleasant walking experience is enhanced by visits to islands normally inaccessible during high tide.

The West Coast Trail was originally forged to save the lives of shipwrecked mariners and follows the rugged shoreline with topography ranging from sandy beaches to rocky outreaches. Wide ledges, caves, tidal pools and waterfalls add to the variety and difficulty of the trail, which has become legendary for being a tough hike from start to finish. You can go at your own pace and pick the part you like!

The Broken Group Islands, an archipelago of more than 100 islands, is situated in Barkley Sound, a favourite area for ocean kayakers and canoeists. The area has a thriving undersea environment, complete with many shipwrecks, which also makes this a popular destination for scuba divers.. Oh, and you just never know when you'll see a whale!

Long Beach, Pacific Rim National Park. A. Cornellier/Parks Canada/10.104.03.18.106

Killer whales off Pacific Rim National Park. P. Mercier/Parks Canada/10.104.10.03.05

Windswept point on South Beach in Pacific Rim National Park. Parks Canada/10.104.03.28.16

Long Beach Wayne Lynch/Parks Canada/10.104.07.19.25

Day and night views of the British Columbia legislative building with statue of the city's namesake, Queen Victoria.

VICTORIA

Victoria's magnificent inner harbour with the landmark, Empress Hotel at left and the British Columbia legislative building at right.

Victoria, British Columbia. More British than Britain? Some who live here might say so but the capital of B.C. is quintessentially alive with British flavour. Blessed with the best climate in the country (winter?, what winter?), Victoria is all that is Britain, from the English Gardens to the architecture, from the cobblestone streets to the tea rooms, from the double-decker buses to the horse-drawn carriages. Like many of Canada's western cities, Victoria was founded in 1843 as a Hudson's Bay Company, British fur trading post. In 1868, it became the capital of the newly joined crown colonies of Vancouver Island and British Columbia.

For years, its harbour was the major centre for commerce and trading on the west coast. But when the railway came to Vancouver in 1882, the pace of life in Victoria slowed down some and things remain pretty much the same to this day! The harbour is a centre for trade and the fishing and logging industry. Tourism here is huge. The British legacy is everywhere, in massive stone buildings, quaint cottages and Victorian-era government buildings. But all is not quite as it seems in this colourful setting. Another culture has also left its mark. Totem poles, the most visible symbol of the west coast's first inhabitants, are prominently displayed throughout the city, reflecting this dual heritage.

Canada's Pacific coast is like a super-highway for migrating whales. These magnificent creatures winter in the warm waters off the coast of Mexico and South America and in the summer, head back to the rich feeding grounds of northern British Columbia and Alaska. During the summer months, hundreds and hundreds of orcas, grey and humpback whales can be seen all along the coast of Vancouver Island. Local tour guides identify many of the whales in their area, naming their favourites, and every spring, for 20 years or more, they look forward to the return of their friends. If you're going whale watching on either coast of Canada the big whale watching boats are great, but nothing beats the experience of getting "up close and personal" in a zodiac type of craft.

Totem park.

Killer Whale breaching, Strait of Juan de Fuca.
Dale Sanders / Masterfile

SNOWBIRDS

Internationally respected as one of Canada's foremost goodwill ambassadors and instrumental in armed forces recruiting, the Snowbirds have become a Canadian institution and a treasured national symbol. Like the RCMP's Musical Ride, the Snowbirds perform for millions of spectators every year across Canada and the United States. Their distinctive nine-plane show, along with the unique ability of their Tudor jets to remain "onstage" throughout their demonstration, make them unique in the world of military jet teams. Bomb bursts, head-on solo passes, cross-overs, rolls and loops – their exciting brand of flying has won the Snowbirds fans around the world.

A nine-plane Diamond Formation of the famous 431 Air Demonstration Squadron better known as the "Snowbirds", over the Comox Glacier on Vancouver Island.

Inset, Snowbirds over Parliament Hill in Canada's capital city of Ottawa, Ontario.

RCMP

In 1874 an initial force of 274 Mounted Police trekked 900 kilometres across the prairies to establish law and order in the Canadian west. The "March West" included no draft horses. Saddle horses pulled the field guns that some men called "horse killers" / Robert Magee

Everyone wants his or her picture taken with a Mountie! Canada is the only country that can claim their national police force as one of their greatest tourist attractions! In 1873, the Dominion was quickly expanding west. In May of that year, the Parliament of Canada passed an act creating the Mounted Police Force for the Northwest Territories. The southern part of those territories would become present-day Alberta and Saskatchewan. The purpose of the force, to be called the North West Mounted Police, was to establish law and order in the frontier reaches of what was quickly becoming a vast nation.

The opening of Canada's wild west under the Northwest Mounted Police was in stark contrast to what was happening in the United States. The NWMP took a peaceful approach, using force only as a last resort. In the process of settling the American west, the U.S. Army massacred thousands of Indians. There is no such blemish in the Canadian history books. In fact, the Canadian government's decision to outfit the force in their British-like red serge was directly related to staying away from any likeness of the U.S. Army's dreaded "blue coats".

RCMP Inspector Walsh leading a small detachment of Mounted Police into the camp of Chief Sitting Bull, where the Sioux had settled after defeating Custer's cavalry at the battle of Little Big Horn. "In the Land of the Mounted Police" / Robert Magee

Located at Fort Walsh, this bronze by John Weaver commemorates the formation of the North West Mounted Police (today's RCMP)

Members of the RCMP's Musical Ride observe the ceremonial flag-lowering in the golden glow of a setting sun at the end of their moving Sunset Ceremony, held every Spring in Ottawa.. *(See photograph overleaf)*

Undermanned from the word go, but always finding a solution and getting the job done, NWMP personnel are legendary. Shortly after the Battle of Little Big Horn, and the defeat of General Custer, Sitting Bull and the Sioux people moved into Canadian territory. Superintendent James Morrow Walsh and Sitting Bull forged a diplomatic relationship and the Sioux' stay in Canada remained peaceful.

The reason for the surprising success of the Mounted Police is to be found in their simple code that was to have one law for everyone and that, when they made a promise to the First Nations people, they would honour it.

After establishing law in the quickly populating territories, the NWMP was presented with another challenge. Little had been heard of the Yukon prior to 1886, but a gold strike on the Fortymile River, just inside the Canadian border, changed everything. The government quickly dispatched a 200-man force of Mounted Police who afforded assistance and protection and maintained the peace with little loss of life for the tens of thousand who entered the Yukon searching for gold.

In 1904, King Edward VII granted the prefix "Royal" to the unit, and in February of 1920, the Mounted Police absorbed the scandal-ridden Dominion Police, which had carried out policing in eastern Canada. Headquarters was moved from Regina to Ottawa and the force became known as the Royal Canadian Mounted Police.

Today, the RCMP, with their brilliant red serge tunics, Stetsons and black polished boots, are part of Canada's heritage and national identity. Since 1901, the RCMP Musical Ride has been a public symbol of the force and has entertained millions worldwide. The highlight of the ride is the famous, "Charge!" (page 4) when lances are lowered and riders and their mounts launch into full gallop, with hoofs thundering and the audience cheering them on. From that initial complement of 275 men, the RCMP of today numbers over 14,000 and provides policing to all provinces and territories. with the exception of Ontario and Quebec. The RCMP remains the national police force of the country, serving government wherever needed, and smiling for photos whenever asked!

Members of the Ride training at 'N Division', their home base in Ottawa.

One of the sure signs of spring in the nation's capital of Ottawa is the annual Sunset Ceremony performed by the RCMP Musical Ride. Split-second timing ensures that, with the completion of their performance. the ceremonial flag lowering coincides perfectly with the setting of the sun.